on track ...

Nick Cave
& The Bad Seeds

every album, every song

Dominic Sanderson

SONIC**BOND**

sonicbondpublishing.com

Sonicbond Publishing Limited
www.sonicbondpublishing.co.uk
Email: info@sonicbondpublishing.co.uk

First Published in the United Kingdom 2022
First Published in the United States 2022

British Library Cataloguing in Publication Data:
A Catalogue record for this book is available from the British Library

ISBN 978-1-78952-240-2

Typeset in ITC Garamond & ITC Avant Garde
Printed and bound in England

Graphic design and typesetting: Full Moon Media

on track ...

Nick Cave
& The Bad Seeds

every album, every song

Dominic Sanderson

sonicbondpublishing.com

Acknowlegements

My thanks must go to all the many journalists and biographers who have interviewed, reviewed or written about Cave during the many stages of his career – reading such material has been immeasurably helpful. Obviously, I must also thank Nick Cave and The Bad Seeds for composing some of the best music the world has to offer.

I am very grateful for the help and support given to me by my parents – without such encouragement, I wouldn't be where I am today.

Finally, I would like to thank Stephen Lambe at Sonicbond Publishing for this amazing opportunity.

on track ...

Nick Cave
& The Bad Seeds

Contents

Introduction

At the age of 64 (at the time of writing), with a successful career well into its fifth decade, Nick Cave is still very much active and at the top of his game. In 2020, he responded to COVID-19's debilitating effect on the live music scene with an arresting live album that captured an isolated Cave performing a career-spanning set reworked for only voice and piano in London's Alexandra Palace. In 2021, Cave and current Bad Seeds co-writer Warren Ellis released *Carnage* – their first non-soundtrack studio album, and the first album of new music from Cave since the Bad Seeds' *Ghosteen* in 2019. In 2021 – after completing a UK tour with Warren Ellis (showcasing music from *Carnage* and *Ghosteen*) – Nick Cave and The Bad Seeds released *B-sides & Rarities Part II*, chronicling the band's swift change in musical direction from the garage-rock-inflected *Dig, Lazarus, Dig!!!* through to the ambient soundscapes of *Ghosteen*: the album that completed a three-part trilogy in which Warren Ellis became the main influence over the Bad Seeds sound. He inherited Mick Harvey's position, who up until *Dig, Lazarus, Dig!!!* was the band's beating heart since the world was graced with their debut album *From Her to Eternity* in 1984.

Despite the fact that Cave's musical career is evidently far from over – the completion of the Bad Seeds' ambient trilogy symbolising their new (and perhaps continued) direction, and the second part of their latest B-sides album cementing this new period further – it feels like a good time to reflect on how they began. They were one of the most important post-punk and alternative rock bands to dominate the 1980s and 1990s, wrestling with different identities in the 2000s, only to arrive in the 2010s with a new and refreshing electronic sound.

It was out of the ashes of Cave's violent punk outfit The Birthday Party, that the Bad Seeds were formed. With co-founders Mick Harvey and Blixa Bargeld being the only stable members during the 1980s, the band took on a new persona that, in time, would increasingly contrast with The Birthday Party's abrasive noise and shocking live antics. Despite this, the Bad Seeds' 1980s output is – unsurprisingly – some of their most brutal, fuelled by Cave's obsession with the cruel and merciless God of the Old Testament, and a chaotic lifestyle characterised by heavy drug use. Their most successful 1980s album *Tender Prey* (1988) is a good example of that. It was also the decade in which Cave established himself as an actor and an author – he featured in the 1988 film *Ghosts... of the Civil Dead*, and his first novel *And the Ass Saw the Angel* was published in 1989: its themes of madness, death, obsession and depravity perhaps encapsulating this period of The Bad Seeds the best.

The 1990s heralded a new, happier and rehabilitated Cave, living in São Paulo, Brazil, with his new wife Viviane Carneiro. With that, the Bad Seeds became softer and more piano-driven for their first 1990s album *The Good Son* (1990). The band returned to this understated sound at the end of the decade for their most critically acclaimed album *The Boatman's Call* (1997), but for opposing reasons: a failed affair with British singer PJ Harvey, and a return to the drugs, left Cave heartbroken at the decade's end. In between these albums, The Bad Seeds produced some of their most successful and identifiable work, including *Let Love In* (1994) and *Murder Ballads* (1996). If the Old Testament characterised the 1980s, it was the New Testament that inspired Cave during the 1990s, along with an increased fascination with the concepts of love and of course, death: which was still a central subject!

The 2000s is perhaps the strangest Bad Seeds period to describe, as they appeared to markedly change their identity with each new release. *Nocturama* (2003), in particular (often cited as their weakest album), suffers from an identity crisis, and consequently sounds a little cobbled together. This was also the decade in which founding members Harvey and Bargeld left the band. Despite the losses, the decade's final release *Dig, Lazarus, Dig!!!* (2008) was hailed as a return to form – its garage-rock-inspired sound being a close sibling to the successful eponymously-titled debut from Cave's new project Grinderman.

But this was to be the Bad Seeds' final *rock* album, as Warren Ellis – armed with his synthesizers – became Cave's right-hand man. Three elegant albums define The Bad Seeds' current electronic period: a three-part trilogy that begins with *Push the Sky Away* (2013) and is completed by their latest album *Ghosteen*. The Bad Seeds' most-recent two albums are particularly poignant due to the unexpected death of Cave's son in 2015. Although most of *Skeleton Tree* (2016) was written prior to this tragic event, the immediacy of Cave's grief can be felt; whereas the content on *Ghosteen* – the first album written in the aftermath – is more joyous and uplifting: a grief considered but not altogether eliminated. With each new release, the arrangements are more sparse, and the music takes on a greater fluidity. For me, the entire trilogy is some of the Bad Seeds' best work, along with their mid-to-late 1990s output. This will probably not be the final offering we get from The Bad Seeds, but for now, their multifaceted career has been neatly wrapped up.

Nick Cave – Man or Myth?

It was with the Holy Trinity Cathedral Choir in the small Australian city of Wangaratta that Nick Cave made his recording debut in 1971 – as part of a live recording of 'Silent Night' and 'O Little Town Of Bethlehem': an innocent start to a recording career that would properly accelerate with Cave's first major band The Boys Next Door. Cave first encountered bandmates Mick Harvey and Phill Calvert at Melbourne's Caulfield Grammar School for boys – a more harsh and antagonistic world compared to Wangaratta, which he described in Mark Mordue's *Boy on Fire* biography as a 'magical place, where only good things ever happened'. Cave brought to Caulfield Grammar a reputation for being a tearaway – developed at Wangaratta High School – and consequently brawled with many of the bigger students. Despite his rebellious nature, he was highly intellectual, his father having introduced him to literature at an early age and Nick later obsessed over great works such as Vladimir Nabokov's *Lolita* and

Fyodor Dostoevsky's *Crime and Punishment*. Nick and his father often entered heated debates concerning literature – Nick putting forward his own theories and ideas in an attempt to compete with his father's knowledge.

Cave was also a talented artist, and in 1975 after his secondary education, he began a fine arts course at Caulfield Institute of Technology with the intention of becoming a painter. His preference for 16th and 17th-century renaissance and gothic religious art over 20th-century art brought criticism from his art teachers, not that Cave really cared. Despite this conflict of opinion, he did well in his first year, with a painting style heavily influenced by Australian artist Brett Whiteley. However, Cave's heightening interest in pornography began to make itself clear in his second-year work. One teacher, in particular, told him she couldn't relate to sleazy art. From that moment on, it became Cave's mission to rile her with his profane art style as much as possible. He ended up failing his second year as a consequence, and a thoroughly disheartened Cave cut his education short and left Caulfield Tech in 1977. Later – in 1987 – he suggested it was his time at art college that contributed to his hatred for all critics.

In the year Cave quit his education, a punk outfit named The Boys Next Door (made up of Cave, Mick Harvey, Phill Calvert, Tracy Pew and John Cocivera (albeit briefly)) made their live debut at a church hall in Ashburton: taking their first steps into the world of music. It was a good time for them to do so – Australia was slow to absorb the new overseas music, with music magazines and import records arriving three months out of date, and, therefore, no longer current and trending. The growing power and energy of the DIY punk philosophy aimed to counteract this problem. Furthermore, Australia's leading bands of the underground music scene (The Saints and Radio Birdman) had left for the UK in the middle of 1977, leaving an empty space for The Boys Next Door to effectively fill.

Australian label Mushroom Records were keen to take advantage of the punk scene, and Barrie Earl set up the country's first subsidiary punk label, Suicide Records: an Australian version of the successful UK label Stiff Records. Along with a few other punk bands, Earl instantly signed The Boys Next Door and became their manager. After only six professional shows, the band found themselves signed to a label and preparing to record their first single – a cover of Lee Hazlewood's 'These Boots Are Made for Walkin'' – released in March 1978, and later recycled on the *Lethal Weapons* compilation released the following May (which also featured the original songs 'Boy Hero' and 'Masturbation Generation', and tracks from other bands). But the compilation was a flop, and by the end of 1978, Suicide had dissolved, and all their bands had broken up except for The Boys Next Door.

In the process of Suicide's demise, the band reluctantly spent time with producer Les Karski, recording their proposed debut album *Brave Exhibitions* and gained a new band member in the form of guitarist Rowland S. Howard from The Young Charlatans. Unhappy with the resulting recording, Mushroom compromised and allowed the band to record new tracks with producer Tony

Cohen, who instantly hit it off with The Boys Next Door, unlike previous producers. The end result was their debut album *Door, Door*: released in May 1979. Side one featured Cave's compositions from their sessions with Les Karski, and side two showcased Howard's material recorded with Tony Cohen. In a 1979 interview with Michael Faber of *Farrago*, Melbourne University's student magazine, Cave said, 'The first side is basically a rock 'n' roll sort of record, and the second side is far more adventurous'. Indeed, Howard's song 'Shivers' became the anthem of the Crystal Ballroom – a venue that The Boys Next Door regularly played in the run-down St Kilda area, where the chaotic bedlam of the group's later incarnation, The Birthday Party first sprouted. Unfortunately, *Door, Door* sold a poor 2000 copies, but it represented another necessary step towards the sound they were after.

By the end of 1979, the band had signed with Keith Glass' Missing Link label, and they finally felt at home. Their first release there was the *Hee Haw* EP in December 1979. According to Cave in a 1979 *Roadrunner* interview, '*Door, Door* was controlled, tame, stilted, organised and heavily structured', but *Hee Haw* was a Pere Ubu-influenced affair with dissonant textures and a yelping, snarling Cave. The band had begun to find an identity with this more arty, experimental direction, and Glass believed it was time for the band to find success in England.

At their final Crystal Ballroom gig, the band gave away a new single titled 'Happy Birthday' as a parting gift before they left for England. It is also the first song to be included in Cave's *Complete Lyrics* book (2001), suggesting that what had come before was unworthy. With a new chapter about to begin for the band, a new name was needed, and they unanimously agreed to call themselves The Birthday Party. This was the beginning of the end for the band formerly known as The Boys Next Door – The Birthday Party lasting for only three years due to increasing tension and differences within the band. But in those few years, they succeeded in creating a true name for themselves as 'The Most Violent Band in Britain': as advertised at a Cologne gig on their 1981 European tour. Their live performances were a horrifying spectacle, described beautifully in a 1981 *Sounds* review as 'a mixture of paranoia, demented self-parody and neurotic inebriated passion'.

It was the band's arrival in London in 1980 that sparked their desire to shock and terrify their audience. Along with the squalor and poverty they were forced to endure, Cave spoke of the stagnant atmosphere of the UK live music scene in a 1981 *NME* interview: 'Coming to London has been one of the most disillusioning experiences of my life ... because when we came here, we thought here at least people were doing more than standing around twanging their guitars'. A music video for their first single, 'Nick the Stripper', showcased the violence and derangement the band were keen to bring to their live performances in order to combat the inaction of UK audiences.

Their first album *Prayers on Fire* was released to great critical acclaim in April 1981, and its abrasive sound mirrored the band's on-stage antics. Right from their debut, The Birthday Party had found their voice. The second single, 'Release the Bats' was issued in July, cementing the band's status further, earning the title of fan favourite, and becoming a great influence on the emerging gothic rock scene. However, the single's recording process had heightened the rift between drummer Phill Calvert and the rest of the band, who were becoming dissatisfied with his polished rock 'n' roll style. Mick Harvey was responsible for writing Calvert's drum parts for him, and this was only the start of a sharper descent for the band.

A UK and US tour followed, the latter being of particular interest. The debut album had only been released in San Francisco on a small label, so they were relatively unknown in America. Similar to UK audiences, the US' docile response to The Birthday Party prompted the band to be as manic and violent as possible. Consequently, during the second US show, the venue pulled the plug halfway through due to the band's absurd antics. In response, other US venues then decided to cancel the band's shows. However, it was those first two shows that suddenly made the US aware of their existence.

On their return to the UK, The Birthday Party encountered completely different audiences to those on their first UK trip. The audiences now flung themselves at the band in an attempt to be the craziest and most daring: a complete turnaround, to the dismay of Cave. The band continued to reside in London as they toured the US and Europe whilst making occasional trips back to Melbourne.

In 1982 on their second European tour, The Birthday Party struck up a lasting friendship with their German support band Die Haut. Cave was also formally introduced to Einstürzende Neubauten singer Blixa Bargeld, who later became an important member of Nick Cave and The Bad Seeds.

In July 1982, the second Birthday Party album *Junkyard* was released, attaining positive reviews. Mick Harvey described it as 'our warped vision of rock' in Ian Johnston's *Bad Seed* biography, which is a fair judgement considering the general endeavour to mistreat studio equipment and make the most heinous of sounds during the album's making. Some of Mick Harvey's drum contributions further highlighted the band's distaste for the traditional rock 'n' roll style represented by Phill Calvert, who was becoming dissatisfied with the band's sound. The band's instability was made greater by bassist Tracy Pew – a chaotic individual who was arrested and jailed during the album sessions for driving drunk – leaving Barry Adamson (who was to be part of the Bad Seeds' first lineup) to record some of the album's bass parts.

Junkyard can be considered a transitional album, involving as it did the imminent departure of Phill Calvert, the band's relocation to Berlin (where their friends Die Haut and Einstürzende Neubauten were), and the changeover from Cave and Rowland Howard as the main songwriters, to Cave and Harvey. This was clearer on the follow-up, *The Bad Seed* EP, released in February 1983, on which all songs are Cave/Harvey co-writes. The band told the press that their music was too intense for the LP format. Despite accusations of misogyny and fascism (due to the front cover's swastika), the EP gained critical acclaim, and Howard believed it was The Birthday Party's most focused record.

Their final release – the *Mutiny!* EP – is 'a documentary of the group in utter collapse', according to Cave. The band were now signed to Daniel Miller's Mute label (Depeche Mode's label), but the *Mutiny!* sessions came to a halt with only seven tracks recorded. After only six weeks on the Mute label, Harvey left the band. The remaining members agreed to finish the EP later in the year before the band toured Australia. But things became sour in Melbourne, where their concert was labelled 'The Last Birthday Party Concert'. In reality, the final Birthday Party concert had taken place in June 1983 at the Crystal Ballroom: the very place where the band started out.

In August, the band regrouped to finish the *Mutiny!* EP, and Roland left the sessions on bad terms with Cave. So, The Birthday Party was no more – its appetite for destruction being ironic considering their own self-destruction. In September, Cave began recruiting for a solo project with the intention of recording a three-track EP titled 'Nick Cave – Man or Myth'. Mick Harvey was the first person to join the ranks, followed by Blixa Bargeld and Barry Adamson. This eventually became the first lineup of Nick Cave and The Bad Seeds.

From Her to Eternity (1984)

Personnel:
Nick Cave: vocals
Mick Harvey: guitar, drums
Blixa Bargeld: guitar
Barry Adamson: bass
Anita Lane: (credited but does not play)
Hugo Race: guitar
Jim Thirlwell (uncredited): bass
Recorded at Trident Studios, London (Side A) in March 1984; The Garden Studios, London (Side B) September-October 1983
Producers: The Bad Seeds, Mark Ellis (Flood)
Label: Mute Records
Release date: 21 May 1984
Chart positions: UK: 40, USA: -
Running Time: 43:22

In a *Rolling Stone* interview conducted in November 1983 – shortly following the demise of The Birthday Party – Cave seemed reluctant to re-enter the music industry: 'I'm mainly interested in diversifying as much as possible. Doing projects. Being in a group and working to make that group successful is over'. That same month, Cave agreed to write a screenplay for videomakers Evan English and Paul Goldman which would be based on the narrative of the Birthday Party song 'Swampland'. Little did Cave know that this would be the beginnings of a project he would later reshape into his debut novel *And the Ass Saw the Angel*, propelling his art into the literary world. Little did he also know that he'd find success with a new musical group, despite his assertion that his time working to make a group successful was 'over', achieving success beyond what he was probably aiming for at that time, and it all began with *From Her to Eternity*.

Sessions for the Bad Seeds' debut album began early in 1983 at Garden Studios in London – before the first Bad Seeds lineup was solidified and before Cave's solo venture had even taken that band name. Harvey, Bargeld and Jim Thirlwell were also present at these sessions, in which four of Cave's compositions (that were to appear on the album) were worked on: 'Saint Huck', 'Wings Off Flies', 'A Box For Black Paul' and 'From Her to Eternity'. However, due to artistic differences between Cave and Thirlwell, Thirlwell was quickly replaced by Barry Adamson – Cave's friend who'd temporarily been the substitute for Tracy Pew during the making of *Junkyard*. These new sessions came to an inconclusive end in October 1983.

Before Cave's return to London in March 1984 – to continue work on the album at Trident Studios – a select few of the yet-to-be-released songs were played live by Cave's band, which included Harvey, Adamson, Pew and Hugo Race (who filled the role Bargeld was unable to accept due to his duties with Einstürzende Neubauten). Songs such as 'A Box For Black Paul' and 'Wings Off

Flies' were played alongside songs from *Mutiny!*. This was a band moving from the demented chaos of The Birthday Party to a softer, more narrative-based affair that would allow Cave's lyrics to shine, and these live appearances made this transition clear.

The album was released in May 1984, during the Bad Seeds' first European tour. The album received widespread praise, with Mat Snow in the *New Musical Express* calling it 'one of the greatest rock albums ever made'. While Snow would later revise this bold statement, there's certainly a case for the album's strength as a debut. Though the approach here is softer in comparison with the chaotic noise of The Birthday Party, there's still a violent brashness present that hearkens back to those early days. Cave still sounds as demented as he did on those earlier records – his yelps and screams helping to communicate the disintegration of his depraved characters.

The contribution of Anita Lane – Cave's girlfriend until November 1983 – cannot be understated. She co-wrote the lyrics for a number of the Birthday Party songs, and after her death in April 2021, Cave called her 'the brains behind The Birthday Party' (*The Red Hand Files*, issue 146), highlighting her importance in enabling the band to progress into the Bad Seeds. Though she does not play anything on *From Her to Eternity*, Lane's influence was significant in the shaping of Cave's sinister characters and their grim stories: hence she is credited on the album.

The accompaniment is just as captivating as Cave's centre-stage narratives. Pushing the boundaries of tonality, Bargeld's guitar work is coarse, disjointed and wonderfully bizarre. Not only does he inject an avant-garde flavour, but instead of an all-out assault on the ears (as one might expect from a Birthday Party song), Bargeld plays sparingly, in turn giving the music much-needed space for Cave's vocals to shine. In fact, there's an overall sense of coherence and strategy here that's absent from those Birthday Party records. Cave somewhat waves goodbye to the old, to usher in the new whilst retaining the Birthday Party spirit, and he does it rather effectively.

'Avalanche' (Leonard Cohen) (5:13)

Cave's interpretation of the late Leonard Cohen's 'Avalanche' is excitingly original and haunting. The album *Songs of Love and Hate,* from which the song was taken, played a crucial role in the development of Cave's taste in music and describes it as being Cohen's greatest record. It was also a source of lyrical inspiration, with the opening track 'Avalanche' being particularly powerful as Cave explained in *Boy on Fire*: 'The first track 'Avalanche' was the most extraordinary lyric I'd ever heard – still is, really. For me, doing it as the first song on *From Her to Eternity* was as much a calling forth of my childhood years in Wang as a tribute to the master poet songwriter.'

Upon hearing the tribute, Cohen commented in a 1993 *Seconds* interview that Cave had 'butchered my song 'Avalanche', and if that's the case, let there be more butchers like that'. It had Cohen's approval, and it also has mine. The beauty and fragility of the original in all its glory is ruthlessly stripped away by Cave, the butcher, to reveal something more gruesome and sinister beneath. The original's warm acoustic guitar and lush strings are replaced with dread-provoking piano, Adamson's booming bass, Harvey's creeping drum fills and the sound of Bargeld's abrasive electric guitar, foregrounded by Cave's psychotic vocal. If the original is more of an outward cry for help, this version despairs quietly in a corner somewhere.

'Cabin Fever!' (Cave, Bargeld) (6:11)
As a fine example of a track that wouldn't be anomalous if included on a Birthday Party record, this claustrophobic and relentless storm of a song leaves no breathing room. The sonic field is packed with a variety of sounds fighting to be heard – many of these being Bargeld's industrial scrapes and clatters that bombard the listener. Cave's vocal delivery is perhaps the most deranged here – his shrieks and wails communicating the frustration of an isolated sea captain entrapped on a ship that doesn't appear to be sailing anywhere. Near the beginning, we hear of the captain's upper-arm tattoo, which reads 'A-N-I-T-A': a reference to Cave's ex-girlfriend Anita Lane. Much like their tumultuous relationship, the ship's aimless course is anything but smooth, the journey's choppiness reflected in Adamson's fretless bass work and the track's descending chromatic figure that relentlessly repeats throughout.

'Well Of Misery' (Cave) (5:25)
In keeping with the previous track's pirate/sailing theme, the group's call-and-response vocal chants might remind the listener of a sea shanty. But it becomes clear that Cave's characters are at work. Harvey's severe percussion playing on the downbeats throughout is reminiscent of someone being whipped or a hammer hitting something. This is monotonous work, reflected in the song's lack of musical development – Adamson's bass and Harvey's hits providing a sparse and repetitive rhythm section against the vocals. Occasionally there are glockenspiel interjections, and as the track closes, there's a tasteful harmonica solo which really adds to the blues sensibility. While this isn't a standout track by any means, it showcases Cave's love of blues music: an influence absent from the post-punk noise of The Birthday Party.

'From Her To Eternity' (Cave, Lane, Bargeld, Race, Harvey, Adamson) (5:33)
As many fans will agree, the title track is the highlight of the album. It's an all-time fan favourite and a staple of the band's live repertoire. For Cave, the feeling is mutual, as explained in a 2004 interview included in an expanded chapter of Debbie Kruger's *Songwriters Speak* book:

> I guess it's one of my favourite songs that I've written, as a piece of music, especially, and have great joy in playing live … I remember writing that sitting

up in bed with Anita Lane. She helped me write that, and conceiving this notion that the object of desire is being up on the next floor, and all of the connotations of that. I thought the recorded version of it was extraordinary. I'd never heard anything like Blixa's guitar in that song, and I've never heard anything like it since, from anywhere. It's just so out there. It's so powerful, but it's basically piano-driven.

The piano is indeed the track's beating heart, driving forward Cave's discomforting tale of a character's perverse obsession with the girl in the room above him. The piano works hard in communicating the self-inflicted torture of his unattainable desires through those jarring, violent chords that really challenge the C-minor tonality outlined in the piano's lower register – I think it's probably fair to use the word dissonant. Similar to the technique used in 'Cabin Fever!', Bargeld's background scrapes, scratches and other unworldly guitar noises help to create a sense of claustrophobia, successfully emphasising the protagonist's downward spiral into madness. This desire, and the potential fulfilment of desire, turns murderous: 'But ah know that to possess her is therefore not to desire her/Oh, Oh, Oh then ya know, that li'l girl would just have to go'. For Cave, once desire – the thing that brings us pleasure – is realised, 'the desire is gone, and so is the pleasure'. With pleasure gone, the girl is no longer of use to our protagonist, and she will just 'have to go' – the multiple layers of Cave's intertwining guttural screams making for a barbaric and chilling ending that points towards the girl's murder. This is a very grim tale – so much so that PJ Harvey (who Cave was to encounter down the line) said in a 1992 *Spin* interview that 'it made me feel physically sick' on the first listen. I could almost say the same, but Cave's character development and the murderous twist at the end – all effectively framed by the dissonant aural carnage – make for an incredibly captivating listen.

'Saint Huck' (Cave) (7:22)

This was the first track the Bad Seeds recorded, and it's just as monstrous as the one preceding it. When you hear Cave's spitting delivery of the word 'achtung', you know the track's begun – its relentless, march-like pursuit underscored by Adamson's repeating bass line and Harvey's snare rolls. Of course, Bargeld litters the track with his cacophonous variety of background noises. And to make sure the listener is feeling thoroughly tense, the doom-laden piano will surely have you on the edge of your seat. It's the perfect musical accompaniment to Cave's brooding subversion of Mark Twain's *Huckleberry Finn*. The protagonist is not the well-natured doer of good deeds that we encounter in Twain's novel but is on an opposite path leading to corruption and depravity. The 'dirty ol' man latrine' – the stinking sinful swamp that Saint Huck wades through – is symbolic of his depravity. Cave later incorporates the sinful swampland into his debut novel – a swampland that instils fear in the religious-manic Ukulites who seek redemption from an unmerciful god. In fact, included on the album's inner sleeve is a short prose piece titled 'The Black Pearl': a precursor to Cave's narrative epic. I will refrain from saying any more about the novel at this stage, but by the end of this song, Saint Huck is unable to save himself from his descent into depravity and eventually ends up being shot in the head.

'Wings Off Flies' (Cave, Thirlwell) (4:06)

This is the only compositional contribution from Jim Thirlwell, before he departed due to creative differences between him and Cave. It's also the album's shortest track and perhaps its weakest. Again, it showcases Cave's love of the blues, the slide guitar being most indicative of the blues sensibility here. Apart from the track's sharp, dynamic contrasts, there is nothing musically extraordinary to point out. However, the lyrics are once again rich in subversion – an innocent children's activity is turned on its head into something brutal and violent, in which the wings of flies are plucked out on the saying of 'She loves me, she loves me not', instead of petals. But if you're able to decipher the rest of Cave's nonsensical scrawl, it may make you giggle, despite the song's underlying malevolence.

'A Box For Black Paul' (Cave) (9:42)

In contrast, this is the album's longest track, and is an exquisite closing epic that will leave you exhausted. It's reduced to just Cave's vocal accompanied by a spectral piano, with subtle additions from Bargeld. The narrative is particularly poignant here – Cave's funeral speech for Black Paul – who was lynched – is arguably a representation of The Birthday Party's demise. After all, The Birthday Party share the same initials as Black Paul, and both are looking for some sort of closure: 'Who'll build a box for Black Paul?/And who'll carry it up the hill?/Who'll bury him in the black soil?'. Cave's yelps, screams, screeches and unholy wails are absent here. Instead, he narrates with clarity and sorrow. It's Cave himself who 'builds a box' for The Birthday Party, not only closing the Bad Seeds' debut album but closing that chapter of his life and burying it for good.

Related Tracks:
'In the Ghetto' (Mac Davis) (4:06)

This was the Bad Seeds' first-released single and was eventually included on a reissue of their debut album. When the band started gigging, this piano-led cover – originally recorded by Elvis Presley – was performed at every show. If the track's soft ballad-like temperament stands in stark contrast to everything else on *From Her to Eternity*, the subject matter is appropriately dark and miserable, as the song becomes stuck in a cyclical pattern of children being born in the ghetto: a hole of despondent poverty which provokes criminal behaviour in adulthood. This isn't the only time that Cave's Elvis obsession would be exposed through the Bad Seeds' music.

The Firstborn Is Dead (1985)

Personnel:
Nick Cave: lead vocals, harmonica
Barry Adamson: bass, guitar, organ, drums, backing vocals
Blixa Bargeld: guitar, slide guitar, backing vocals, piano
Mick Harvey: drums, piano, guitar, organ, bass, backing vocals
Recorded at Hansa Tonstudio, Berlin: November-December 1984
Producers: The Bad Seeds, Flood
Label: Mute Records
Release date: 18 June 1985
Chart positions: UK: 53, USA: -
Running Time: 40:37

The Bad Seeds' second album saw them venture even further from the post-punk noise of The Birthday Party, which was at least an underlying presence on *From Her to Eternity*. With the group reduced to a four-man unit due to the departure of Hugo Race (who wanted to pursue a solo career), the Bad Seeds began to test out new Cave compositions on their October 1984 European tour. These songs would eventually be recorded for *The Firstborn Is Dead*. The heavy blues influence on these new tracks – an influence that poked its head through on songs from the debut such as 'Well Of Misery' and 'Wings Off Flies' – alienated those fans who weren't prepared for the band's sharp direction change.

Having again relocated to Berlin (The Birthday Party's dwelling place, and a welcoming city that had 'this creative, artistic scene' according to Cave), the Bad Seeds recorded their follow-up album. In comparison with their frightening debut, the blues replaced the punk attitude; gone are Cave's deranged yelps and screams, and gone are the saturated, claustrophobic soundscapes. Subtlety and dynamics are used to a greater degree here in order to convey the moody blues.

To match this new direction, Cave's lyrics were heavily imbued with his fascination for the American Deep South – an influence that bled into his lyrics as a result of writing his novel, which was in the throes of construction throughout the 1980s while he recorded with the Bad Seeds: 'It was about an imaginary religious community in the Deep South, so I started reading the Old Testament. And it drew me in. It took me back to childhood. I used it as the bedrock for the novel', exclaimed Cave in a 2009 *Mojo* magazine interview. Simultaneously digesting the genius of Southern Gothic writers like William Faulkner and Flannery O'Connor, Cave's obsession with the cruel and rancorous God of the Old Testament really became apparent on *The Firstborn Is Dead*, pervading Cave's work for the rest of the 1980s.

Upon the album's release, it failed to garner the praise the debut did. One review in particular aggravated Cave to the extent that he, in response, wrote a B-side called 'Scum' (released later in the decade). Mat Snow had been the critic who hastily glorified their debut as the best rock record he'd ever heard but commented that a new Einstürzende Neubauten single, 'musters the psychodramatic edge disappointingly absent from Nick Cave's forthcoming LP'. Snow's erraticism – and a host of unfairly-negative reviews – heightened Cave's disliking of the media. The album perhaps suffered from negative reviews as a consequence of the album's delayed release due to the band waiting on Bob Dylan's approval of their cover of his 'Wanted Man', which the band had drastically altered and added to. It meant that the band had to tour with a mishmash of players who were unfamiliar with their new material – including The Birthday Party's Rowland S. Howard – without having released the album yet. This gave the media an excuse to pick on Cave and the new album.

That all being said, overall, this album is one of their weakest. Discounting the opening track, there are no other standout moments, and certainly none as powerful. Most of the tracks merge into one due to the album's monotony. A change in direction is always a welcome thing from any band, and this album was a necessary one in the Bad Seeds' development. On *The Firstborn Is Dead*, this is a band yet to master the sound that would pack more of a punch on their later 1980s albums.

'Tupelo' (Adamson, Harvey) (7:17)

A storm, the Old Testament and Elvis Presley – indeed, these are the three main ingredients included in what is perhaps the band's most powerful album opener. It has proven to be another enduring Bad Seeds classic, frequently taking its rightful place in the concert setlist. It's often cited as one of the best songs to come out of Cave's 1980s period – which is strange considering the same compliment can't be made for any of the album's other tracks. Casual fans either refer to the album as 'the blues one' or 'the one with 'Tupelo' on it'!

A clamorous thunderclap introduces Adamson's juddering bass line, Bargeld's jangling blues guitar, Harvey's tribal tom work and Cave's ambitious reimagining of the birth of our Lord and saviour: Elvis Presley. Yes, in Tupelo, Mississippi, on a dark and stormy night, the flood story of the Old Testament is made real, as the town is deluged in 'Water, water everywhere/Where no bird can fly/Where no fish can swim'. On this night of judgement in a tin shack, Elvis 'the King is born', second after the firstborn, who dies the next morning. This is based on Elvis' actual birth, at which his firstborn identical twin brother Jesse was stillborn. And now we know where the album title comes from.

If you read *And the Ass Saw the Angel*, you'll find many parallels between the God-like birth of Elvis and the birth of the novel's main protagonist Euchrid Euchrow. For example, in the novel, the flood is a constant reminder of when Euchrid is born of God's oppression. But in this case, it's based on the John Lee Hooker song of the same title, that is based on the Great Mississippi Flood of 1927. This is a town in desperate need of saving: made clear in the refrain 'O God help Tupelo!'. It's a long and painful cry that recurs throughout Cave's seven minutes of artful rambling. For a song of this length with only two chords, it goes to show just what a masterful storyteller Cave already was.

'Say Goodbye To The Little Girl Tree' (Harvey) (5:10)

From here on, the album suffers from a familiar blues monotony that's never quite as formidable as the raging powerhouse opener. The energy is certainly reduced on this track, which has a more stereotypical blues swing complete with slide guitars. Apart from occasional moments of crescendo, the groove is unwavering as Cave outlines the tale of a father's pain letting go of his daughter as she outgrows the innocence of youth.

'Train Long-Suffering' (Cave) (3:49)

This is another track that doesn't waver in its course, but here the journey is frantic and fast. Despite the relentless driving rhythm, this train is heading for 'destination, misery' on 'rails of pain and suffering': in other words, it's going nowhere. It utilises a call-and-response between Cave and the Bad Seeds' gang chants. But, once again, an unremarkable track, in contrast with the onslaught of the opener.

'Black Crow King' (Bargeld, Cave) (5:05)

A similar formula used in the debut album's 'Well Of Misery' is adopted here – a sparse arrangement, chain-gang responses to Cave's calls, and percussive hits emphasising beats one and three. Bargeld's sorrowful blues guitar initially demands attention equal to the vocal, before Adamson's fragmented bass enters with the percussion. The sustained and languid sound of an eerie Hammond organ adds to the overall sense of brooding.

The story here is a simple one: about a scarecrow that reigns over the corn field day and night in all weathers. It is again a stormy night, and everybody has gone. It's no surprise that Cave has taken on the persona of the Black Crow King, with his long black hair, his dark suits and his ability to scare people.

'Knockin' On Joe' (Cave) (7:38)

One of the album's better moments, this slow-blues piano ballad is the longest track here, and one of the most affecting. Cave's crooning is most solemn as his protagonist faces the reality of being a prisoner on death row. The American prison system is something Cave took a great interest in during the 1980s, and would research it further for the 1988 prison-focused film *Ghosts... of the Civil Dead*. He also made his most grand and definitive statement on the American prison system in the song 'The Mercy Seat', near the end of the band's 1980s phase. But there's less of a statement here and more just a sense of complete hopelessness and despair. For example, the song title is an American slang term for prisoners avoiding manual labour through self-mutilation – a morbid reality made clear in the line 'These hands will never mop your dirty death-row floors'. The metallic clink of Bargeld's guitar, the moan of Cave's harmonica and Harvey's understated drums all grow in intensity towards the climax: a final hopeless wail from Cave's protagonist.

'Wanted Man' (Bob Dylan) (5:27)

As Cave had already established on the Bad Seeds' debut opener 'Avalanche', he really knew how to make a cover his own. This Bob Dylan cover (originally written for Johnny Cash) is no exception, as Cave not only completely alters the song, so it barely resembles the original, but he goes one step further and extends Dylan's lyric with his own. Dylan's delayed response in giving permission for the song's use was the reason the album release was delayed while the Bad Seeds did a promotional tour for the album, despite nobody having heard it yet!

There is a greater sense of urgency here compared to the original; the unceasing quaver rhythm resembling the running motion of a man trying to escape the countless American states and cities (including Tupelo) from which he is wanted. Throughout, it feels like it's building towards something, but by the end, there's no climax; no resolution. Rather, it just seems to fritter off.

'Blind Lemon Jefferson' (Cave, Bargeld, Harvey, Adamson) (6:10)

Along with 'Knockin' On Joe', this is, for me, the album's only other highlight after the initial punch of 'Tupelo'. Based on the bluesman of the same name and telling of the blind man's death in a ditch, this track plunges you into the ambient menace of the blues. Cave paints a rather grim picture of Jefferson's death, his body being pecked at by crows who 'slap a death-writ on his door' as he awaits the 'Judgement train'. However, his road is 'dark and lonely' – an inevitability that's perfectly encapsulated in the hazy atmosphere. The bass is deep and dark, the vocal reverb is haunting, the rhythm guitar quiet and jittery, and the tempo is incredibly slow. Musically, this suggests that Jefferson is in a state of limbo. By the end, the song's only chord change emphasises the final lines – 'If that sky serves as his eyes/Then that moon is a cataract' – which in turn highlights the non-resolution of this spiritual existence in limbo.

Kicking Against the Pricks (1986)

Personnel:
Nick Cave: lead vocals, organ, piano interior
Mick Harvey: piano, backing vocals, acoustic guitar, bass, drums, guitar, co-lead vocals, snare drum, vibes, string arrangements
Blixa Bargeld: guitar, slide guitar, backing vocals, co-lead vocals
Barry Adamson: bass, backing vocals, co-lead vocals
Thomas Wydler: drums, percussion
Guest musicians:
Dawn Cave: violin ('Muddy Water')
Hugo Race: guitar ('Hey Joe', 'Long Black Veil' and 'I'm Gonna Kill That Woman')
Tracy Pew: bass ('Hey Joe')
Rowland S. Howard: guitar; organ ('By the Time I Get to Phoenix'); co-lead vocals ('All Tomorrow's Parties')
Berliner Kaffeehaus Musik Ensemble: strings
Recorded at AAV Studios, Melbourne, November-December 1985; Hansa Tonstudio, Berlin, March 1986
Producers: Tony Cohen (backing tracks), Flood, The Bad Seeds
Label: Mute Records
Release date: 8 August 1986
Chart positions: UK: 89, USA: -
Running Time: 45:28

After the poor reception that *The Firstborn Is Dead* received – a rather unwarranted media trampling – Cave's next move was brave and wholly unexpected considering the band were in their early-career stage. In order to antagonise the critics he so loathed and because of the demands Cave faced with his novel, Cave and the Bad Seeds released the aptly titled *Kicking Against the Pricks*: an album made up entirely of covers. Whilst the title is a phrase taken from Acts 26, Verse 14 of the King James Bible, it's undeniably more synonymous with an upset Cave kicking against those critics that had ever said a bad word about the Bad Seeds. 'I suspect I might be one of those pricks', wrote Mat Snow after a smug Cave showed him the track 'Scum' during an unfruitful *NME* interview in 1986 regarding the cover album. When explaining the reason for doing a covers album, Cave stated simply and bluntly: 'There was no round-table debate as to what each particular song means. When I listen to a song, it strikes my heart whether it's worthwhile or not. There's something so basic and so simple, it shouldn't even need to be said'.

Instead of giving the press a meandering tale bathed in deep contemplation, Cave spoke the simple truth. Indeed, some of the chosen covers hearkened back to his childhood days of musical discovery in Wangaratta. Furthermore, the cover album introduced the Bad Seeds' fan base to genres not yet explored on their previous records – such as gospel, country and western, and what Cave called 'entertainment' music: Tom Jones and Gene Pitney, for example. There is the familiar blues that pervaded their previous album, but there's also a reshaping of identity here, in which the band cast off the chains of the gothic post-punk identity associated with The Birthday Party. This creatively liberating album allowed Cave to really assert his influences and the band's potential future.

This was the first record to feature long-time Bad Seeds drummer Thomas Wydler, who has appeared on every Bad Seeds album since and is still with the band. They were also reunited with producer Tony Cohen, who last worked with them four years previously when they were The Birthday Party, and he was someone that had the band's approval and trust. He worked with the band up until 2001. But though the album was recorded with bassist Barry Adamson, he departed from the band just before the album was mixed, in order to concentrate on a solo career.

Once the album was released, it was to Cave's great surprise that it received widespread praise beyond anything laudatory of their previous output. Ironically, he'd accomplished the opposite of what he desired and had done it with flying colours. For an album demoted to consisting of covers due to the excuse of Cave's novel, it's just as important as any other Bad Seeds album, if not more. It gave the band an opportunity to stylistically improve as a unit, and according to Harvey in a 2009 *Record Collector* interview, the album was 'part of a process of Nick finding the type of music he wanted to play'. The original music that the band released in the future benefitted highly from the reimagining process of *Kicking Against the Pricks*.

'Muddy Water' (Phil Rosenthal) (5:15)
This is a slower, more downbeat version of Rosenthal's country original. Instead of his lively acoustic guitar strumming, Bargeld's economically palm-muted plucking keeps Cave's moody version steady. With a lush string arrangement – which includes Cave's mother on violin – and a sorrowful piano, this sprightly country classic is transformed into a contemplative ballad.

'I'm Gonna Kill That Woman' (John Lee Hooker) (3:44)
This murder ballad is heavier here, with more bite than Hooker's original. I certainly prefer the dynamics, the chaos of Bargeld's guitar interjections, and the harsh and incongruous vocal over the straight-up blues of the original: which I find to be monotonous compared to this wonderfully-strangled cover.

'Sleeping Annaleah' (Mickey Newbury, Dan Folger) (3:18)
When I first read this was a Tom Jones cover, I couldn't quite place The Black Crow King alongside the Welsh pop legend. In contrast to the album's earlier tracks, this isn't wildly dissimilar to the original. But the main point made here is that Cave's obviously attempting to challenge himself vocally with something melodic that demands more from his range and technique. He may not have the polish of Jones, but Cave does a stellar job. It's precisely this desire to improve that makes the *Pricks* exercise such a significant step.

'Long Black Veil' (Danny Dill, Marijohn Wilkin) (3:46)

Characterised by acoustic guitars and Wydler's upbeat snare rolls, this is quite a jaunty cover of the country classic, exemplifying the band's desire to wipe clean their gloomy post-punk identity. While the chorus vocal harmonies are rather uplifting and contagious, I find the rest of it to be lacking in interest.

'Hey Joe' (Billy Roberts) (3:56)

This is a much more tense and atmospheric take on what became Jimi Hendrix's wailing rocker, though this version is devoid of a growling guitar. Instead, a distant jittering piano outlines those renowned chords, while Cave merely mutters the words Hendrix so purposefully yelled. Wydler's unceasing tom rhythm adds to the overall tension. It's perhaps one of the album's most original covers, not to mention the most cinematic.

'The Singer' (Johnny Cash, Charlie Daniels) (3:09)

A straightforward country cover of the Cash song originally titled 'The Folk Singer'. The beautiful string arrangement is the saving grace here, underscoring the track's recurring guitar motif and Cave's deep, languid vocal until the isolated closing lines, 'Did you forget this fucking singer so soon?/ And did you forget my song?' – the first line altered from Cash's original 'Did you forget this folk singer so soon?'. Cave's alteration – a good overall representation of the song itself – is more sinister than Cash's rustic original.

'All Tomorrow's Parties' (Lou Reed) (5:52)

This is an energetic, fast group sing-along, in contrast to the lackadaisical world-weary charm of The Velvet Underground's original. This is one of two times on the album where Cave looks back on the artists that inspired him in his youth. It's also one of the few times here where Cave cannot match – let alone outdo – the original.

'By The Time I Get To Phoenix' (Jimmy Webb) (3:39)

Jimmy Webb's emotional piano ballad is performed in the context of a full band here. The restrained Hammond organ growls (courtesy of old Birthday Party bandmate Rowland S. Howard) beneath the slow drum groove, simple bass notes and descending guitar lines give an ominous edge as Cave again weaves his way through another vocally-challenging piece.

'The Hammer Song' (Alex Harvey) (3:50)

Not to be confused with the original Bad Seeds' song of the same name on their 1990 album *The Good Son*, Cave here pays homage to his teenage hero Alex Harvey, who spearheaded The Sensational Alex Harvey Band. In the mid-1970s, the Scottish rock 'n' roll outfit 'changed the trajectory of our lives', according to Cave, who, along with his classmates, including Mick Harvey, started out playing Alex Harvey covers (including this song) in the Caulfield Grammar school band.

This haunting cover is masterful, the mellow organ and snare rolls playing a prominent role in building tension throughout. On the original, the tension only comes with the quiet interlude before the breakdown. Here there's no such pause, and instead of the raucous rock 'n' roll breakdown complete with raging lead guitar, Cave's vocal harmonies and ghostly intertwining vocal lines gradually expose themselves and steal the show by the end.

'Something's Gotten Hold Of My Heart' (Roger Greenaway, Roger Cook) (3:44)

Another strange clash: Nick Cave sings Gene Pitney. Along with the Tom Jones number, this is probably the most vocally demanding, with Cave singing at the top of his range at one point.

'Jesus Met The Woman At The Well' (Trad. Arr. The Alabama Singers) (2:00)

You may have to pinch yourself listening to this – the band that spat out the deranged 'From Her to Eternity' and the dense bible-laden 'Tupelo' are now singing gospel? Well, you're not dreaming, and I suppose that's the point: to show that the Bad Seeds are more than just doom-and-gloom post-punk rockers. But be prepared to picture Cave and co. howling out this traditional gospel song with the sun shining down upon them!

'The Carnival is Over' (Tom Springfield, Frank Farian) (3:16)

This uplifting and elegant closing track was originally by Australian folk quartet The Seekers. Cave's version is not as outwardly grand but rather more introverted. The atmospheric jittering background guitar against the shuffling rhythm is a nice contrast. Cave's vocal delivery beautifully exposes the lyric's underlying melancholy, heightened by the background howls.

Your Funeral... My Trial (1986)

Personnel:
Nick Cave: vocals, piano, Hammond organ, harmonica
Mick Harvey: bass, guitar, drums, snare drum, piano, organ, glockenspiel, xylophone, backing vocals
Blixa Bargeld: guitar, co-lead vocals
Barry Adamson: bass
Thomas Wydler: drums, fire extinguisher
Recorded at Hansa Tonstudio, Berlin, July 1986; The Strongroom, London, August 1986
Producers: Tony Cohen, Flood, The Bad Seeds
Label: Mute Records
Release date: 3 November 1986
Chart positions: UK: - , USA: -
Running Time: 42:47

One month prior to the release of *Kicking Against the Pricks*, recording started for what would be the band's most accomplished album yet, before Adamson left the band. A mere three months separates the release of the highly-acclaimed covers album and what was originally a double EP – *Your Funeral* containing four contemplative ballads, and *My Trial* comprising three livelier aggressive songs along with a Tim Rose cover. *Your Funeral... My Trial* owes a lot to the covers exercise, the superb quality of the former as a direct consequence of the latter's experimentation with style and genre.

Though this is one of The Bad Seeds' finest records – a precise and refined amalgamation of everything that had come before – the hasty recording process was less than enjoyable. Along with Adamson's early departure (leaving the multifaceted Mick Harvey to complete the majority of his missing bass parts), drummer Thomas Wydler suffered an arm strain injury during the sessions, leaving him in pain and frustrated with the situation. As a result, Harvey once again stepped in and recorded half of Wydler's drum parts. A lot fell on the shoulders of Harvey and Bargeld in these sessions.

As for Cave, his chaotic lifestyle characterised by increasingly-heavy drug use didn't allow for the most coherent sessions. It was a lifestyle he took with him on tour to promote *Pricks*, just before the release of *Your Funeral... My Trial*. The touring between albums was eventful to say the least; incidents occurring here, there and everywhere as a consequence of Cave and sound engineer Tony Cohen trying to score drugs. Perhaps the most severe of these was Cave's stint in a police cell after being caught in the act of scoring red-handed. Due to Cave's self-imposed entrapment, one of the gigs had to be rescheduled.

The day after the tour ended, *Your Funeral... My Trial* was released. But to the band's dismay, the release was overshadowed by the continued success of *Pricks* – released only three months prior, and given a heavy promotional campaign.

The high opinion of what was perhaps Cave's best 1980s album remained unanimous, as highlighted by Chris Long's 2009 BBC review describing the album as 'a showcase of just what grandeur can be achieved by a speedy-yet-dedicated work ethic, and as fine an opus as Cave has ever produced'. Indeed, there is a real coming of age here in which the band channel everything they'd developed and learnt from on their cover album into creating their first definitive statement. According to Mick Harvey in a 2009 *Record Collector* interview, the importance of this album as a blueprint for the construction of future Bad Seeds releases, cannot be understated:

> Somehow there was a freeing up of what was possible. Certainly, our sense of what we were trying to do or what was possible with the Bad Seeds, gelled with that album. It's one of our favourites; not classics all the way through, but there's a lot of different musical ideas. When we'd done that album, we felt we'd found a way forward that we could keep working with ... *Your Funeral...* gave us a template to work on, whereas the first three albums probably didn't.

The band had finally found the classic Bad Seeds formula that would reap the grandest rewards going into the 1990s. The world of Cave's sprawling and all-consuming story bled into the narratives of each track on the double EP, more so than on *The Firstborn Is Dead*. The inner psyche of the main character Euchrid Euchrow is indirectly exposed in parts of the album, and the gloomy world of endless suffering and pain that Euchrid and his fellow characters inhabit is also echoed on certain tracks. Although this sounds thoroughly dark and twisted, the Bad Seeds' most monstrous album, *Tender Prey*, was yet to follow.

'Sad Waters' (Cave) (5:00)

The first EP of the two consists of four slow tracks. This achingly beautiful love ballad is perhaps Cave at his most heartfelt up to this point. His vocal is crisp and clear; the two separate emotive melodies carrying the same lyric, intermingling. In fact, everything here is very clean in comparison to previous Bad Seeds tracks – the guitar is unsullied, jangling innocently in the background, the Hammond organ is dreamy, and instead of the bass being used as a tool of deep, dark dread, it plays melodically in its higher register. Despite the simple tale of loss and reminiscence, this has become another timeless Bad Seeds classic.

'The Carny' (Cave) (8:01)

From gentle memories of one now lost, we descend into the morose world of 'The Carny' – its grotesque carnival dirge characterised by the suppressed growl of the Hammond organ emphasising its nightmarish waltz. Throughout its relentless eight minutes, it alternates between two sections. The first is more intrusive, utilising playful yet sinister xylophone and glockenspiel parts along with Harvey's dissonant plucking of piano strings wired around a metal frame! The second section takes a step back, retaining the feel with a dizzying bass part, but now Cave unleashes his ghastly tale concerning the death of a 'bow-backed nag' named Sorrow that belongs to the carny. After the burial, the rain comes 'hammering down', and the rotting carcass of Sorrow is brought to the surface for the rain and crows to decimate further – there is perhaps no Cave song more miserable.

A true Cave fan will spot that Sorrow appears in *And the Ass Saw the Angel*, the nag there belonging to the family of the main protagonist Euchrid Euchrow. The nag's fate is no better in the novel. Moreover, the eternal rain of 'Tupelo' returns: a symbol of suffering and unattainable redemption for the citizens of Ukulore in the novel.

The band performed the song (along with 'From Her To Eternity') in the 1987 Wim Wenders film *Wings of Desire.*

'Your Funeral... My Trial' (Cave) (3:56)

This is another masterpiece of balladry along with 'Sad Waters', but with a little more punch and vocal grit. Tracks like these hearken back to the covers of 'Sleeping Annaleah' and 'By The Time I Get To Phoenix' from the *Pricks* album. The arrangement is similar to 'Sad Waters', though the Hammond organ sounds whinier, and the piano plays a more prominent role, foreshadowing the piano-led material that was to characterise future albums such as *The Good Son* and *The Boatman's Call*. The lyrics are ambiguous and hard to decipher, but it seems to tell of multiple encounters with prostitutes: 'A thousand Mary's lured me/To feathered beds and fields of clover'. One interpretation suggested that the prostitute's memory of the encounter instantly died (hence 'your funeral'), whereas the customer judges himself, and has to wrestle with the moral implications of this dalliance (hence 'my trial'). Accurate or not, it's an interesting take on Cave's purposefully-vague lyrics.

'Stranger Than Kindness' (Anita Lane, Bargeld) (4:47)

The lyrics of Cave's ex-girlfriend Anita Lane here encapsulate her melancholy feeling of being 'a stranger to kindness' in the aftermath of her separation from Cave.

Bargeld's relentless shivering guitar coil is unsettling in its unresolvable tension, aided in its sinister course by atmospheric background guitar interjections and other strange noises. Cave's numb, monotone vocal delivery is made all the more haunting through an intermingling whispered vocal echoing Lane's affecting words. It's chilling yet glorious!

Interestingly, this song title was used to name Cave's 2020 book. It gives valuable insight into his creative world, complete with reproductions of original drawings and lyric sheets.

'Jack's Shadow' (Cave, Harvey) (5:41)

Here begins the more-fierce energised second EP, on which the quality suffers a little in comparison to its forerunner. 'Jack's Shadow' will be more familiar to fans of the band's previous output, this being a track that could've easily been included on *The Firstborn Is Dead*. Propelled by the furious bass part and rapid three-note guitar pattern, the track ignites straight away, driving forward until it bursts into its clamorous chorus on the repeated line 'And the sun it shined'. Again, the narrative is odd, but in simple terms, it seems to suggest that prisoner Jack Henry is separated from his shadow, which is 'spat from the dirty dungeons', and becomes a wife before Henry tracks it down. He is so burdened by his shadow – 'a shackle from which my time is never done' – that he ends up peeling 'his own shadow off in strips' in an act of irrational desperation. Cave was here influenced by Jack Henry Abbot's *In the Belly of the Beast* – a book made up of Abbot's letters detailing his experience of the merciless American prison system: this may help anyone wanting to decipher the narrative further.

'Hard On For Love' (Cave) (5:19)

If the last song presented a complex narrative with potential for multiple interpretations, this is quite clearly one of aggressive sexual yearning communicated through biblical language:

> I am his sceptre and shaft
> And she is Heaven and Hell
> At whose gates I ain't been delivered
> I'm gonna give them gates a shove

This discomforting mix of the profane and the sacred is something Cave took a great interest in, keeping his own personal notebook of images forcing the sacred and profane together. The artwork for each EP also showcased this unusual pairing – an image of St. Veronica on the inner sleeve of *Your Funeral* is forced alongside a drawing on the *My Trial* inner sleeve where a woman uses a hand mirror to inspect her genitals.

The pent-up frustration of this sexual yearning is musically communicated through the aggressive, snarling bass line, the unceasing screeching background drone and the infectious group chorus that repeats the title. Cave's vocal intensity increases until he becomes primal by the track's close.

'She Fell Away' (Cave) (4:30)

This is not as overtly sexual but nonetheless opens with 'Once she lay open like a road'. In another tale of difficult loss, the protagonist descends into a state of suicidal thought. The music in 'Sad Waters' and 'Stranger Than Kindness' reflects their similar themes of loss, but here a playful piano rhythm is retained, galloping alongside a chirpy xylophone part. There is also apparently a fire extinguisher here (used by Wydler), though it must be subtle as I can't hear anything that sounds like one.

'Long Time Man' (Tim Rose) (5:35)

Cave's cover of this Tim Rose song is unremarkable. It lacks the distinction of the other tracks and is not that different from the original. But the narrative suits Cave – Rose telling of a man in prison for killing his wife and regretting it ever since. In fact, Cave's treatment and depiction of women generally on the album caused critics to level the accusation that he was a misogynist: 'I just find there's essentially something more exciting about seeing women being abused' exclaimed Cave in a 1987 *National Student* interview. But Cave relished the attention, and proudly admitted it, even being called The Misogynist in a Bad Seeds tour brochure, which was probably out of spite towards the critics, rather than a genuine confession of misogyny, but it's something Cave continued to be questioned about throughout his career.

Tender Prey (1988)

Personnel:
Nick Cave: vocals, Hammond organ, piano, vibes, harmonica, tambourine
Mick Harvey: bass, bass loops, piano, guitar, backing vocals, xylophone, drums, acoustic guitar, percussion, Hammond organ
Blixa Bargeld: slide guitar, guitar, backing vocals
Kid Congo Powers: guitar, backing vocals
Roland Wolf: piano, Hammond organ, guitar, backing vocals
Thomas Wydler: drums, backing vocals
Guest musicians:
Hugo Race: backing vocals ('Mercy'), guitar ('Watching Alice')
Gini Ball, Audrey Riley, Chris Tombling: strings ('The Mercy Seat')
Ian Davis: backing vocals ('Slowly Goes the Night')
Recorded at Hansa Tonstudio, Berlin; Vieklang, Berlin; Trident, London; The Strongroom London, August 1987-January 1988; 'Mercy' and 'Alice' recorded by Chris Thompson at The Studio, Richmond
Producers: Tony Cohen, Flood, The Bad Seeds
Label: Mute Records
Release date: 19 September 1988
Chart positions: UK: 67, USA: -
Running Time: 54:34

The pinnacle of Cave's 1980s period, *Tender Prey* was laboriously constructed under the most chaotic of circumstances. When recording began in 1987, it was a confusing time for the group, now joined by guitarist Kid Congo Powers of The Cramps and The Gun Club. Things began rather well when in February, they were filmed performing 'The Carny' and 'From Her To Eternity' for Wim Wenders' film *Wings of Desire*. But the group were relatively inactive for the rest of the year, except for a few live dates and the fragmented recording sessions which began in September. Cave's manager at the time – Jeanette Blecker – was partially to blame for this, feeding Cave with false promises of rewarding government grants when in reality all she was interested in was indulging her romantic fantasies by attaching herself to him. Her disorganisation made her unpopular with the rest of the band. Nevertheless, Cave was also a factor contributing to the band's inactivity, as he'd thrown himself into multiple artistic ventures, meaning he couldn't be entirely devoted to the Bad Seeds. For example, he was still in the throes of writing his novel *And the Ass Saw the Angel*, albeit its completion was near, and he was about to start editing the mammoth narrative. In addition, he was preparing for his acting debut – playing the role of the deranged, ranting inmate Maynard in John Hillcoat and Evan English's Australian prison drama *Ghosts... of the Civil Dead*: a key role that was 'written for Nick' according to Evan English. Cave had also been instrumental in the script writing, and though the film went in a slightly different direction to his original concept, his contribution was important nonetheless. Cave's feelings of irritation and discontent with the prison system and 'the whole apparatus of judgement, people deciding on other people's fates', are further explored on 'The Mercy Seat': the opening track of *Tender Prey*.

Perhaps the most significant factor affecting the recording of *Tender Prey* was Cave's drug addiction, which had started to interfere with the creative process for the first time. The sessions – which lingered on into 1988 – took place at multiple studios, and the atmosphere was less than pleasant. Cave and Tony Cohen – deep in the inescapable pit of their addiction – were often hours late to the sessions due to illness caused by their inability to score heroin. This all came to a head at one session in which Cave punched Cohen on the nose for increasing the volume in Cave's headphones to an unbearable level.

To Cave's horror and frustration, his addiction was also making its way into media coverage. One critic in particular – Jack Barron of the *NME* – antagonised Cave with an incessant line of questioning regarding his addiction and the wider world of drug culture in Berlin, which Barron tried to insinuate Cave had purposefully influenced. Cave cut their first interview short, but the second again ended abruptly when Barron brought up the dreaded subject. In retaliation, Cave threw a glass at Barron's head – the glass shattering on impact – before assaulting Barron further outside on the street. Barron's melodramatic 1988 *NME* article that appeared in the assault's aftermath spewed lines such as 'All I want is to get out of this damned city and never have to look at Cave and his dish-rag limbs again'. Contrary to Barron's accusations, Cave was very much against the idea of being an idol for others in terms of his addiction: 'I really think drugs are quite an evil thing, and I really wished I hadn't become involved with them myself'.

I'm sure that sentence whizzed through Cave's head when he was arrested for the possession of 884 mgs of heroin during the January 1988 *Tender Prey* sessions. In order to avoid prison time, he had to show proof he was making an effort to get clean – and to do that, he had to go to a clinic. His addiction and participation in drug dealing forced Christoph Dreher to evict Cave from his apartment, bringing an end to Cave's stay in Berlin. The city that, in Cave's eyes, had brimmed with creative freedom in the early-1980s had now lost its charm. Relocating to London, Cave escaped a prison sentence, and participated in a detoxification programme at the Broadway Lodge Clinic in Weston-super-Mare.

Just before Cave emerged clean from the clinic, *Tender Prey* – the band's 'monsterpiece' as I like to call it – was finally released. The album – created under such strained and difficult circumstances – was hailed by all. Where *Your Funeral… My Trial* opted for consistency and cohesion, *Tender Prey* went for diversity – each song having its own distinct identity and style that contrasted with the next. In the Barron interview, Cave said, 'Rather than rectify this disjointedness, we decided we'd play on what would normally be a weak point within a record, and make it its strength'. It was a gamble that paid off, even if Cave thought it was a 'piece of shit' during the recording and was still unconvinced by its success after his time in the clinic: describing it as 'one long cry for help'.

A 12" EP of Cave reading extracts from his completed novel was included with initial album copies, again inextricably linking his arcane novel with his 1980s musical output. The novel – finally released in 1989 to great critical acclaim – would be the final nail in the coffin of this most chaotic period: putting the Old Testament to rest, as the Bad Seeds entered a new period. *Your Funeral... My Trial* and *Tender Prey* stand out as Cave's most accomplished 1980s albums.

'The Mercy Seat' (Cave, Harvey) (7:17)

The immensity of this opening onslaught cannot be understated. Arguably the best Bad Seeds track to come out of the 1980s; this monster has been unleashed at almost every Bad Seeds gig since its release. If you want to sum it up briefly, Cave gave it a good go in a 1988 *Melody Maker* interview: 'It has a religious, monastic chant going over an incredibly powerful pulsing thunder sound'. Indeed, that sound is what inspired the track's construction – the cyclical chords and chanting melody arising from tape loops of the cacophonous sound of drumsticks hitting a bass guitar. Along with piercing, galloping strings that grow in intensity on the repeated chorus, the storm of sound is all-encompassing, with an imminent sense of foreboding and doom.

Within this frame, Cave examines the inner psyche of a prisoner on death row awaiting execution as he faces the wrath of God's judgement: 'God is never far away'. The song title is an Old Testament reference – the mercy seat being the throne of God over the Ark of the Covenant, which is paralleled with the electric chair the protagonist will suffer in:

In Heaven, his throne is made of gold
And the ark of his testament is stowed

Down here it's made of wood and wire
And my body is on fire

The parallel serves to show the protagonist's intimacy with God – God is with him and judging him as he suffers 'Down here', which has Hellish connotations. In the final round of choruses, the gradual process of his suffering is made explicit – beginning with 'My head is burning', changing to 'glowing', 'smoking', 'melting', and finally, 'boiling', as each painful chorus lyric relentlessly repeats and develops. His innocence throughout is left unclear, from the early line proclaiming he's 'nearly, wholly innocent', to that ambiguous final line 'But I'm afraid I told a lie'. Whether he's simply lying when he says he's 'not afraid to die', or if he's unsure of his own innocence is vague and left up to the listener to decide. But what *is* clear, is he's fed up 'with all this measuring of truth' – or, in words stated earlier on, fed up with 'people deciding on other people's fates'. This is one of Cave's richest lyrics: full of ambiguity and a breeding ground for countless interpretations.

'Up Jumped The Devil' (Cave, Bargeld, Harvey, Wolf, Wydler, Powers) (5:16)

Similarly dark to the opener, but in a more lighthearted, slapstick manner, this track's vaudeville-style casts Cave as some sort of mad villain. Complete with spiky piano, playful xylophone and an immeasurably catchy sing-along chorus, the track is just as mischievous as the character it portrays: 'Doomed from the start/Doomed to play/The villain's part'. He asserts that 'the righteous path' is 'too narrow for the likes of me', at the same time questioning the identity of a certain other character in the song: 'Who's that yonder laughing at me?'. We all know that it's the Devil, waiting to drag him 'down ... to eternity'. It's almost like a pantomime, albeit a more twisted one.

'Deanna' (Cave) (3:45)

This is a great example of the album's disjointedness, as it moves towards charged garage rock based on Edwin Hawkins' 'Oh Happy Day'. In contrast to the upbeat and rather jolly feel, the lyric is as dark as you'd expect. It refers to an intense relationship Cave once had back in Melbourne as explained in a 2004 interview included in an expanded chapter of Debbie Kruger's *Songwriters Speak* book: 'Lyrically, it talks about that excitement of young love without any responsibilities, where you feel you could just do anything. That's not necessarily anything good, it's anything bad as well'. And in this song, anything means murder, as Deanna is shown how to use a gun – 'Yes, you point it like a finger/And squeeze its little thing' – their youth represented by the childish instructions. Reminders of Hell return in the refrain – 'I ain't down here for your love or money/I'm down here for your soul' – in which Cave inhabits another Devil-like character who exists 'down here' and wants to consume her soul; her everything.

If the album is disjointed *musically*, there's certainly lyrical consistency up to this point.

'Watching Alice' (Cave) (4:01)

This gentle piano ballad communicates Cave's self-confessed fascination for voyeurism. It's lyrically straightforward – the narrator watches and describes Alice as she dresses and brushes her hair at the window: in effect, we, the listeners, also becoming the voyeurs. Cave's fascination is further reflected in his novel's main character Euchrid Euchrow, whose life exists on the 'periphery of things' as he spends 'the entire time recording what goes on in the town that he lives in'. The track is incredibly effective in its ability to entrance the listener; the spell of Cave's drowsy vocal only being broken with a harmonica solo at the close.

'Mercy' (Cave) (6:22)

Another ballad, but less lackadaisical and more melodramatic. St. John the
Baptist – 'thrown into a dungeon' – desperately pleads for mercy: based
on the biblical event in which Herod imprisons him for reproving Herod's
divorce from his first wife. Like the previous track, the piano takes the lead,
but there's a strong drum rhythm throughout; the distant-sounding harmonica
interjections invoking a sense of despair. The instrumental preceding the
final verse is captivating, its increased tempo and drive indicating that time is
running out for John the Baptist. Cave reworks the biblical event so that John
watches himself die over and over again: 'My death, it almost bored me/So
often it was told'. As with every Cave character seeking redemption, John the
Baptist's pleading goes unrewarded. Along with the opener, this poignant and
vulnerable ballad of desperation is a definite highlight.

'City Of Refuge' (Cave) (4:48)

The City of Refuge is the sanctuary where all of Cave's characters on the album
scramble to enter. Influenced by and appropriating the chorus of Blind Willie
Johnson's blues song of the same name, these lyrics could well be aimed at
characters such as the death-row prisoner or John the Baptist, as an unmerciful
God malevolently repeats 'You better run to the City of Refuge'. However,
there's no point running to such a haven, because 'The blood won't wash
off'; sin can never be undone, and therefore, redemption is unattainable.
There is a sinister sadism in the lines, 'When you're dragged toward the Hell
mouth/You will beg for the end/But there ain't gonna be one, friend'. This
is emphasised by the music's fast snarl, which almost feels like a humorous
comic representation of these poor characters running towards something
that doesn't exist. I love the lyrical concept being developed, but musically this
track is not as strong as what came before it.

'Slowly Goes the Night' (Cave) (5:23)

This an odd one. Every track here is to some extent twisted, dark and wicked
towards its helpless characters. But here, we encounter a rather ordinary love
song detailing a breakup, possessing a rather radio-friendly pop sensibility. It
does feel a little incongruous, which may sound contradictory, bearing in mind
that the album's strength is drawn from its disjointed nature. I can find ways of
connecting the other tracks, whereas I really struggle to do so here: this is not
to say that it's a bad song.

'Sunday's Slave' (Cave) (3:40)

This and 'Slowly Goes the Night' are the album's weakest songs, though this
one is not as anomalous. Fuelled by countrified piano and acoustic guitar,
we're back on the course of the twisted and dark: 'Our sufferings are countless/
Our pleasures are a motley few'. But the true meaning of the track, I cannot
fathom – it seems to outline the conflict between slave and master, symbolised

in the days of the week: 'Thursday's angered the master/Okay so Friday's gonna pay'. The lyrics are rather obscure, but I wouldn't say it's an essential track.

'Sugar Sugar Sugar' (Cave, Harvey) (5:01)

Cave's misogyny rears its head in this track which tells of a girl becoming involved with a bad man going down an equally bad road towards the 'city of wrong'. The narrator – a self-confessed 'angel of God' – constantly warns the girl that 'that man is bad' and that she had 'better pray'. The song's lowest point is reached when Cave exclaims, 'He will laugh and hang your sheets to see/The tokens of your virginity': a severely uncomfortable moment in which the man takes pride in his depraved work. Cave's babbling is framed by the band's full-on blues throttle.

'New Morning' (Cave) (3:46)

A breath of relief as we reach the final track, which is a soft country gospel, thankfully resplendent and uplifting in contrast to everything horrifying and evil before it. It's a track 'very much like 'Amazing Grace'' according to Cave in a 1988 *Graffiti* interview. Does the prospect of a new day finally offer a glimpse of redemption in which 'There'll be no sadness/There'll be no sorrow/There'll be no road too narrow'? Or does the dawn's sky 'all covered in blood' suggest the opposite?: a foreboding sense of future pain and suffering. The mystery is tantalising, but this is the closest the album ever gets to redemption.

The Good Son (1990)

Personnel:
Nick Cave: vocals, piano, Hammond organ, harmonica
Mick Harvey: bass, acoustic guitar, vibraphone, percussion, backing vocals, guitars ('The Hammer Song')
Blixa Bargeld: guitar, backing vocals
Kid Congo Powers: guitar
Thomas Wydler: drums, percussion
Guest musicians:
Roland Wolf: piano ('Lucy' reprise)
Clóvis Trindade, Rubinho: vocals ('Foi Na Cruz')
Alexandre Ramirez, Altamir Téa Bueno Salinas, Helena Akiku Imasoto, Léa Kalil Sadi: violin
Akira Terazaki, Glauco Masahiro Imasato: viola
Braulio Marques Lima, Cristina Manescu: cello
Cláudia Ferreti: strings and singer coordinator
Mick Harvey, Bill McGee: string arrangements
Recorded at Cardan Studios, São Paulo, October 1989
Producers: The Bad Seeds, Victor Van Vugt, Flood, Gareth Jones
Label: Mute Records
Release date: 16 April 1990
Chart positions: UK: 47, USA: –
Running Time: 45:12

The new decade saw the dawn of a new Cave. After *Tender Prey* – which quickly became the Bad Seeds' best-selling record – a sober, clean Cave was looking for a new musical direction, as detailed in a 1988 *Graffiti* interview remixed with additional material in 2009:

> I basically want to explore some different themes now. I kind of want my songwriting to be simpler anyway; get away from these incredibly sort of labyrinthine lyrical excursions like 'The Mercy Seat' and things like this. I want the next record to be much simpler, much more a record of songs. It depends on what happens and how they come out, but I want to write some classic-type songs, more singer-oriented songs, possibly like some of the stuff on *Kicking Against the Pricks;* some of the more complicated singing-type stuff. I find I can sing much better these days.

Tender Prey songs like 'Slowly Goes the Night' and 'New Morning' hinted at the vision Cave had for the future. The former song would've probably sounded less out of place on the next album. Little did Cave know when he said this in 1988, that the Bad Seeds would achieve this with flying colours on *The Good Son* – a record created with ease and precision, as opposed to the cobbled-together sessions that made up its predecessor.

After a 1989 US tour in promotion of *Tender Prey*, Cave began to yearn for an escape from the tiresome media that haunted him in London. At one time in Cave's life, London and Berlin had been places that had some sort of allure. But he confessed in a 1990 *Sounds* interview, 'I start to get restless if I stay in one place too long'. The only place Cave hadn't been yet that had the same allure was Brazil. Luckily for him, the Bad Seeds embarked on a brief tour of the country. From the moment he arrived in Rio, he was entranced by every aspect of the city and was unsurprisingly enamoured with the great statue of Christ the Redeemer. But Cave had a greater affinity with the less-tourist-based city of São Paulo – one of the world's largest – which was the most enthusiastic and respectful in welcoming Cave and the group; not to mention that during one of the gigs in São Paulo, Cave locked eyes with art director Viviane Carneiro, and being formally introduced to her after the show, instantly fell in love, despite the language barrier. Cave immediately wanted to stay in this magical place, and ended up spending an extra ten days there after the band left. The pair's relationship blossomed during this time. After these ten days, Cave left for Europe to work on the next album *The Good Son*. With his novel now complete, he was ready to leave behind the twisted, morose themes that previously bled into his Bad Seeds lyrics to work towards the vision outlined earlier on.

Brazil was to have a great impact on Cave's songwriting – an impact that neither London nor Berlin really had. The process of composing in Brazil – as opposed to the strain and frenzy of writing in Berlin or London – was straightforward and joyous, as Cave would sometimes compose whole songs in his head while exploring, and the influence of São Paulo itself found its way into some of the tracks. For the first time, Cave made demos for every song, meaning he'd be able to enter the studio with an organised plan. With this newfound surge of creativity influenced by his surroundings, Cave wanted to take a more prominent role in the studio than he had done previously.

When the band began recording in October 1989 in São Paulo, the whole thing came together naturally. Everything had been planned out. Some of the songs were even layered on the original demo drums. It was a quick, composed affair, which brought Cave some fame in Brazil, as the Bad Seeds were one of the first western rock bands to record in the country. The end result was some of Cave's most lyrically-straightforward, classically-structured songs. They were mostly piano-driven, dealing with themes of remorse and regret. As a result of the album's more understated, melodic direction, Bargeld's guitar experimentation is noticeably spare here – though, as has already been made clear, he was the master of economy; of quality over quantity.

Upon the album's release, Cave was worried about how the album would be received, considering the sharp change in dynamic and tone. But – once again – it was generously hailed as a masterpiece. John Robb of *Sounds* said the album 'rides its luscious toon on a set of simple, heart-wrenchingly romantic lyrics that show a maturity and an honesty glaringly absent in a lot of his contemporaries' guff'. Not only had Cave confirmed that the creative juices were still flowing – even without the *aid* of narcotics – but through *The Good Son*, he and the band separated themselves from the current pop music trends as explained in the same *Sounds* interview: 'I think that on this new record we have finally cut the strings on whatever is happening around us. I don't think that we are reacting to that anymore'. And so, with everything going so well, it's fair to say that everything was rosy in the world of Nick Cave at the dawn of the 1990s.

'Foi Na Cruz' (Cave) (5:39)

We immediately sense Brazil's significant influence on Cave's songwriting, even with the song title. As an adaptation of a Brazilian protestant hymn inspired by the churches of Brazil that explicitly depicted Christ's agony and pain, the chorus translates as, 'He was on the cross/He was on the cross/One day Jesus was castigated for our sins'. We are quickly immersed in Cave's new world, which favours the subdued over the thunderous – characterised by gentle piano, fragile vibraphone and sweet acoustic guitar. In contrast to 'The Mercy Seat' as an opener – with its odd structure and bizarre chord changes – the harmony here is simple, and the structure a straightforward verse/chorus alternation. Where the gospel-like choruses are full-sounding and uplifting, the verses leave more room for the aching strings to shine, as the narrator outlines a lost love, surmising that 'All our grand plans, babe/Will be dreams for evermore'. Overall it's a graceful entrance as light as a feather, which couldn't be more different from *Tender Prey*'s monstrous opening.

'The Good Son' (Cave) (6:01)

Biblical influences remain in a retelling of the Prodigal Son parable. The opening African chant that repeats 'One more man gone', refers to the prodigal son leaving his home in order to squander the inheritance he demanded from his father. The destitute son's return to the celebrations of his father, leaves the older brother – who has always been present – feeling bitter as he 'Lays down queer plans/Against his brother and against his family'. The verse showcases the pent-up resentment through harried acoustic guitar and skittish vibraphone, which build until the tension is released in the chorus on the repeated line 'the good son' – the prodigal son in the eyes of the father, when really it's the loyal older brother who's the good son. The string arrangement in this section is heart-wrenching, soaring to new heights of emotion. Cave manages to piece together three contrasting musical sections to tremendous effect.

'Sorrow's Child' (Cave) (4:36)

Some of the most melodious piano graces this track, which, together with the constant aching presence of the strings, almost brings a tear to the eye. It's a fitting soundscape for a song devoid of hope, in which 'Sorrow's child grieves not what has passed/But all the past still yet to come'. The potential for Sorrow to stand up and overcome such despair is belittled by her child – 'And just when it seems as though/All your tears were at an end/Sorrow's child lifts up her hand/And she brings it down again' – suggesting there will always be sorrow in the future.

'The Weeping Song' (Cave) (4:21)

This was one of those tracks that 'came out of nowhere with very little thought' as Cave was walking from his Brazil home to the bar he frequented. It's become another Cave classic, and many fans would agree it's the album highlight along with 'The Ship Song'. The lyrics are rather brutal, again rendering the prospect of hope unattainable, as both Cave and Bargeld take the mic and communicate universal despair. In a dialogue between father and son, the deep-voiced Bargeld assumes the role of the father, who weeps in despair along with all the other men and women. Cave is then left with the role of the son who has also unintentionally contributed to his father's weeping: 'O then I am so sorry, father/I never thought I hurt you so much'. Future despair is made inevitable through the children who are merely crying; the father reminds his son that 'true weeping is yet to come'.

Despite the rather bleak message, the video is tongue-in-cheek, depicting Cave and Bargeld sailing a sea of tears (made of bin bags) in a rowing boat whilst swigging from cups. Moreover, the music is certainly not as downbeat nor emotionally charged as the previous track. There's a little more bounce and purpose here, the strong rhythm section groove carrying the most responsibility, grounding that wonderfully-catchy melody.

'The Ship Song' (Cave) (5:14)

This is the album's other highlight, and, thankfully, despair gives way to romance. Most likely down to the lovestruck Cave's new relationship with Carneiro, this evocative piano ballad – complete with delicate chimes, warm Hammond organ and the Bad Seeds' gentle singing – conveys the intensity of love. Its imagery is undeniably magnificent:

> Come sail your ships around me
> And burn your bridges down
> We make a little history, baby
> Every time you come around

It's as if Cave is some sort of stranded island, and every time Carneiro passes, she not only makes 'a little history', but comes closer to mooring herself onto this island, promising safety and security. But of course, in true Cave fashion, there's a bittersweet twist, with the lines 'Your face has fallen sad now/For you know the time is nigh': suggesting this intense relationship is coming to an end.

'The Hammer Song' (Cave) (4:16)

Not to be confused with the Alex Harvey cover of the same title on the *Pricks* album, this Cave original is one of the album's more aggressive tracks. His delivery is grittier in comparison to the clean, melodic vocal style on the rest of the album, as he outlines the tale of another outcast son: who leaves home, to the dismay of his parents. Unfortunately, the son's journey is riddled with misfortune – his horse dies; he's nearly killed in a random city, and he begins to see visions of an angel 'with many snakes in all his hands'. He begs for redemption and to be taken back to his 'hometown', framed by a chorus of immense punch as a result of the booming percussion.

'Lament' (Cave) (4:51)

There are very obvious references to Carneiro here, with 'seaside eyes' and 'foreign hymns'. The verses lend themselves to a sort of brooding bossa nova style, complete with trembling strings, playful vibraphone and a syncopated accompaniment. In verse two, Cave layers a whispered vocal track over his main vocal, adding to the overall sense of mystery. In the chorus, this mysterious vibe becomes one of romance, in which the strings become a tool of lush beauty rather than tension. The song is more melodic, and again there's the inevitable parting of lovers: 'So dry your eyes/And turn your head away/ Now there's nothing more to say/Now you're gone away'.

'The Witness Song' (Cave) (5:57)

This is another of the album's few upbeat tracks, yet it's not as gripping. With the constant clatter of drums and the rampant squeal of Hammond organ, it begins and ends in a flurry. A middle section brings the dynamic down, and, in true gospel fashion, the Bad Seeds quietly chant 'Who will be the witness?' repeatedly beneath Cave's ranting. Certain lines – like 'Time gets somewhat muddied here' and 'Who will be the witness when you're all so clean and cannot see?' – reflect Cave's time at the Broadway Lodge clinic. But this has perhaps the album's most ambiguous lyrics, and it's relatively hard to garner a fully-formed idea of what's going on. There's biblical imagery in the image of the 'fountain with the healing powers' that the characters dip their hands into, crying 'Yes, I'm healed', before admitting that they lied. I suppose the song is asking who outside of the clinic stands witness to an individual's healing, but I cannot say for sure.

'Lucy' (Cave, Bargeld, Wolf) (4:17)

This is a closing track of two halves, and it's been posited over the years that it may be about Anita Lane, who appears as the spectral Lucy at 'The end of love/Of misery and woe'. She haunts the protagonist – outlined in the song's first half, which is a heartfelt, reflective ballad. The second half is instrumental, ambient and utterly stunning. Distant shimmering piano underscores delay-effected guitar notes and a sombre harmonica solo to create a most-haunting soundscape: not in a menacing way, but rather to bring the album to a delicate and graceful close.

Henry's Dream (1992)

Personnel:
Nick Cave: vocals, piano, organ, harmonica
Mick Harvey: rhythm guitar, backing vocals, piano, organ, vibraphone, drums, percussion
Blixa Bargeld: guitar, backing vocals
Martyn P. Casey: bass, backing vocals
Conway Savage: piano, vocals, Rhodes, backing vocals
Thomas Wydler: drums, congas, backing vocals
Guest musicians:
Dennis Karmazyn: cello
Bruce Dukov, Barbara Porter: violin
Mick Harvey, David Blumberg: string arrangements
Recorded at Sound City, California, November-December 1991; 'Christina The Astonishing' and 'Loom Of The Land' recorded at Dreamland Studios, New York, November 1991
Producers: David Briggs, Nick Cave, Mick Harvey
Label: Mute Records
Release date: 27 April 1992
Chart positions: UK: 29, USA: -, Australia: 41
Running time: 41:33

If the composing process for *The Good Son* was natural and straightforward, according to Cave in a 1992 *Q Magazine* interview, writing the songs for *Henry's Dream* 'was a complete and utter nightmare', and recording them was not much better. Of all the wonderful gems in Cave's back catalogue, this album is often unfairly overlooked and overshadowed by its companion album *Live Seeds,* a live album which perfectly captured the songs; the studio versions suffering from production issues, as will later be outlined.

Prior to the album's recording, a number of changes had occurred. Whilst touring the previous album, the lineup was altered. Kid Congo Powers left due to commitments with The Gun Club, and to pursue a solo career: which was beneficial for the Bad Seeds, who were not suited to Powers' wild rock guitar. With his departure came two new Australian members: bassist Martyn P. Casey and organist/pianist Conway Savage; the former still a member to this day. Again, this was to the band's advantage, as Harvey could now hand bass duties to Casey in order to focus on lead guitar. Overall, their mutual attitude towards music, aided the band in becoming a more cohesive unit.

Perhaps the biggest change was for Cave, who in May 1991 became a father. Carneiro gave birth to their son Luke, to the delight of Cave, who'd always wanted a child and had a good rapport with children generally. This provoked a change in his outlook as he explained for the *The Observer* in 1992: 'Having him, and being protective and responsible: it hasn't been easy, but you have to take control. I feel more a part of things as well'. Once the outsider, Cave now

45

had to engage with the world and take on new responsibilities. The three of them moved to New York in order for Cave to start work on the next album.

São Paulo had become Cave's sanctuary away from the world of rock – a world which only presented him with the album-tour-album-tour routine he was so tired of. In São Paulo he was allowed to enjoy the simple things such as reading and going to restaurants, and almost every day, he had visited Pedro's Bar – which was a short walk from his home – and struck up a lasting friendship with its owner. Instead of exploring the country, Cave had happily cocooned himself in his home area. It was perhaps the comfort of being away from everything music-related that made the task of songwriting incredibly difficult for Cave in Sāu Paulo after *The Good Son*. It took a visit from Anita Lane when Cave was back in New York, to encourage him to persist with his new musical direction.

Indeed, Cave wanted to veer away from the strict structure and soft temperament characterising the last album's songs in favour of a more aggressive acoustic-based record in which he left it up to the band to interpret the songs however they wished: in contrast to his major involvement in *The Good Son*'s musical direction. The band were often instructed to hammer out just one chord. Other than that, they were free to do whatever they wanted with that one chord, allowing the lyrics – which were more volatile in terms of perspective and ideas – to garner more attention than ever before.

Since the days of The Boys Next Door, the band had vowed to never again use a producer after having multiple bad experiences. However, due to pressure from the label, on this occasion, they appointed David Briggs, who'd previously produced Neil Young. Being open-minded, the band thought the record might benefit from a producer, or at least a named producer might aid the band's popularity in the US. Unfortunately, these hopes were unfounded, and Briggs' raw live-in-the-studio approach – which didn't necessitate the need for many overdubs – didn't work for the band one bit, leaving Cave again infuriated with the process. Furthermore, Briggs' domineering attitude didn't help matters, this often antagonising Cave to the point where he'd challenge Briggs and leave the studio. This would then repeat indefinitely.

Unsurprisingly, the result didn't meet Cave and Harvey's standards: the mix lacking in dynamics and sounding inadequate overall. Henceforth, Cave vowed again to never work with a producer. Consequently, with the help of Tony Cohen, Cave and Harvey remixed the album. Though the remixing went well and the album received excellent reviews, the band later released *Live Seeds* – recorded over multiple tour dates promoting *Henry's Dream* – in order to present some of the songs how they should've been presented on the studio album.

'Papa Won't Leave You, Henry' (Cave) (5:54)

The opening track rivals 'The Mercy Seat', and is a true highlight that showcases the band at their best. The acoustic guitar is dominant, opening with its low growling menace and leading the track's fierce romp; the strings are used with a little more freedom as a way of building tension when the dynamic is taken down. It's a track you can imagine being played in a pub amidst drunken celebrations, with its acoustic drive and gang chants in response to Cave's vocal. This contrasts with the outlined apocalyptic vision in the lyrics: The Brazilian locale in which the song was written, finds its way into the lyrics, from 'the relentless rains' washing away entire towns, to 'death squads' performing random killings: epitomising the line about death leaping out of every door. This world is a pit of horror and threat in which 'The road is hard/And many fall by the side'. However, the impact of Cave's newborn child is undeniably significant to the chorus. He said in a 2009 *MOJO* interview that the song was 'composed more or less completely in my head without writing it down, while standing over Luke's crib. I used to sing that song to him and develop it and make it up'. Represented by Henry, Cave promises his son that he'll stay by his side as they navigate the horrors they may encounter on the road of life. The sound is raw and the words are captivating.

'I Had A Dream, Joe' (Cave) (3:43)

We move from the album's best track to, arguably, one of its worst: a supercharged gallop that always has its foot on the accelerator. In the verses, we hear each stage of the narrator's dream cycle – first, the dream itself, followed by the aftermath, and, finally, the narrator's reflection on the disappearance of Joe: the mysterious individual from the dream. The narrator's disparate dream images – the man in the road foaming at the mouth; a 'Shadowy Jesus' and a 'pimp in a seersucker suit' – are unified in the final reflective verse, suggesting Joe is that shadowy Jesus in a seersucker suit. It's very odd, and I may have misinterpreted it, but the idea of an elusive, disappearing God seems to make sense.

'Straight To You' (Cave) (4:35)

The equivalent of the previous album's 'The Ship Song', this is this album's melancholy love ballad – albeit Cave has written better love songs of a similar temperament. The Hammond organ really shines here, whether in the quieter verses or the dynamically contrasting grandiose choruses, which see electric and acoustic guitar paired for the fullest possible sound. With each verse comes the gradual death of the relationship that the narrator first establishes as being a saviour: 'All the towers of ivory are crumbling', 'This is the time that I'll come running/Straight to you'. By verse two it's already clear from the light in the window fading, that this dying process has begun. And by the time we get to the final verse, 'Heaven has denied us its kingdom': in other words, a happy life cannot be sustained after the death of the relationship.

'Brother, My Cup is Empty' (Cave) (3:02)

Cave's acoustic-led favela punk resumes here as he rapidly unloads a torrent of humorous lyrics. In a bar and in the throes of a drunken stupor, our frenzied protagonist pleads for someone to refill his cup before he has to go home and face his wife, as he claims, 'I haven't got a penny'. He has nothing nice to say about anyone whether they buy him a drink or not; his worst wishes being reserved for his wife: 'For many a night I lay awake/And wished that I could watch her die', 'To watch her groaning in the dirt/To see her clicking tongue crack dry'. It seems the only thing our protagonist values is his whisky: his 'One tiny little blessing/And now that blessing's gone'.

'Christina The Astonishing' (Cave) (4:51)

Dominated by Hammond organ and some very interesting background percussion, this dreamy track tells of Christina, who was presumed dead, but during the Agnus Dei, 'sprang up from the coffin' and ascended towards the church roof in Liege to 'escape the stench of human corruption': a story taken from Alban Butler's *Lives of the Saints*. Revolted by the smell of human sin, Christina 'fled to remote places' for the rest of her life.

This track is not as loved as it should be. I think its haunting after-effect is beautiful, and I find the story to be incredibly fascinating and very much related to the idea of original sin that pervades Cave's earlier work.

'When I First Came To Town' (Cave) (5:22)

Partly based on the Karen Dalton recording of the traditional ballad 'Katy Cruel', this is a poignant reflection on Cave's restless movement around different countries and his changing perceptions. Upon his arrival to town, he's graciously welcomed: 'People took me 'round from end to end/Like someone may take 'round a friend'. But the kindness quickly dissipates to the point where 'Suspicion and dark murmurs surround me'. For example, in Berlin, the media used Cave's notorious drug addiction to explain the city's wider drug problem, to Cave's dismay. By this point, he was becoming disenchanted with his current city, and more isolated due to being neglected by his friends there. But Cave knows the score: 'There is always one more town/A little further down the track'. The music is melodramatic as a consequence of the strings. And I wouldn't call it remarkable, but you'd have to be made of stone to not feel the emotion behind this personal tale of endless rejection.

'John Finn's Wife' (Cave) (5:13)

If the album opener exceeds the other tracks, this one is a close second. The Bad Seeds here merge the opener's acoustic menace with a lush string arrangement evoking a sense of romance. A spluttering Hammond organ adds to this strange-yet-wonderful fusion, and when the track truly kicks into gear, the whole thing is a delight of drama and intensity. It brilliantly encapsulates the passionate desires of the protagonist, who lusts after John Finn's wife, who has 'Legs like scissors and butcher's knives/A tattooed breast and flaming eyes'. When John Finn walks in and catches the protagonist with his hand 'between the legs of John Finn's wife', a conflict takes place that concludes with the protagonist's bolo knife 'in the neck of mad John Finn'. The music is incredibly responsive to the action. With the final verse comes a musical twist, in which all the menace is sucked out, leaving the romantic strings to dominate. Cave merely narrates that verse over the most beautiful uplifting chords, as John Finn's wife 'took all the flowers from her hair/And threw them on the ground'. Is this an act of mourning or freedom? – another tantalising mystery that ends on a major note.

'Loom Of The Land' (Cave) (5:08)

Another haunting ballad that is gently lulled by slow acoustic guitar and piano. There are multiple ways of interpreting the relationship between the narrator and his lover Sally – perhaps they're young and in the throes of love, exemplified by the line 'Her breast it was small and warm in the palm of my hand' and the narrator's plea for her to rest her 'little head' upon his shoulder. But a more chilling and likely correct interpretation casts the narrator as a paedophile, this being apt due to the inadvertent lifting of the line 'The poplars were turning their backs' from Vladimir Nabokov's *Lolita* – the novel exploring the paedophilic desires of the protagonist who becomes obsessed with a 12-year-old girl. Cave read Nabokov's novel endlessly since his father introduced him to it in his youth, and so it's no surprise that Cave unintentionally included a line from it here.

'Jack The Ripper' (Cave) (3:45)

The album closes with a sinister 12-bar blues fuelled by acoustic guitar, the male narrator humorously telling of submitting to his domineering wife, who 'rules my house with an iron fist' and 'screams out 'Jack the Ripper' every time I try to give that girl a kiss'. It's a powerful end to an equally powerful – if inconsistent – album. *The Good Son* is the stronger of the two Brazil albums.

Let Love In (1994)

Personnel:
Nick Cave: vocals, piano, organ, backing vocals, Rhodes, oscillator, bells
Mick Harvey: guitar, backing vocals, organ, drums, bells, tambourine, shaker,
string arrangement
Blixa Bargeld: guitar, backing vocals, vocals
Martyn P. Casey: bass, backing vocals
Conway Savage: piano, backing vocals
Thomas Wydler: drums, tambourine, timpani, shaker, triangle, temple block,
backing vocals
Guest musicians:
Tex Perkins, Rowland S. Howard: backing vocals ('Do You Love Me?')
Mick Geyer, Nick Seferi: backing vocals ('Jangling Jack')
Spencer P. Jones: backing vocals ('Ain't Gonna Rain Anymore')
Robin Casinader, Warren Ellis: violin ('Ain't Gonna Rain Anymore', 'Do You Love
Me? (Part 2)')
David McComb: backing vocals ('Lay Me Low')
Donna McEvitt, Katharine Blake: backing vocals ('Do You Love Me? (Part 2)'
Recorded at Townhouse III, London, September 1993; Metropolis, Melbourne,
December 1993
Producers: Tony Cohen, The Bad Seeds
Label: Mute Records
Release date: 18 April 1994
Chart positions: UK: 12, USA: -, Australia: 8
Running Time: 48:18

One of the quintessential Bad Seeds records, *Let Love In* is the perfect
beginner entry point, as it encapsulates everything that the group are
about, encompassing their varied and unique sound. It was the band's most
commercially successful and highest-charting album to that point.

    After living in São Paulo for two years and recording two albums there,
the inevitable happened – Cave became disenchanted with the city, which
was already made clear on the *Henry's Dream* track 'When I First Came
To Town'. The fact that Cave couldn't learn Portuguese, coupled with his
isolation from the world, had an impact on his ability to easily get through
everyday life. He had a few options: America was one of them, the place
having once creatively inspired Cave. But America was another place
he'd become disenchanted with – its harsh environment and unattractive
societal views being unsuitable. Melbourne was a more-endearing option,
but ultimately, London was Cave's best bet, as his publisher and record
company were based there. Besides, now having the financial stability he
was devoid of on his first arrival in London in 1980, he was now more
enamoured with the city, and he always had the option of returning to
Brazil.

In 1993, Cave, Carneiro and their son moved to North Kensington, and for the first time, Cave faced the prospect of being settled: something that didn't feel natural at first but that he soon became acquainted with. In such domestic bliss, after having spent years running from one place to the next, self-examination was in order, and the outcome of such introspection formed the basis of the next record: his most personal yet.

Nestled away in a bar on Portobello Road, Cave began writing songs for the next record, still characterised by his usual themes of death, loss, and most obviously from the album title, love. Less reliant on using fictional characters, he instead wrote more of himself into the music. By summer 1993, most of the material was written, and recording began with Tony Cohen again appointed as co-producer.

The *Let Love In* sessions were some of the band's most productive ever, despite the enforced speed. Cave set a deadline for the record to be completed before his booked flight back to Brazil. This meant there was no time to lose, and consequently, Cave became incredibly obsessive, writing for most of the day. His fixation was so severe that he listed everything that needed doing, scattering the sheets of paper across the studio. If anyone marked these notes, Cave wrote them up again on a fresh sheet, as they had to stay uncontaminated. Pictures of these notes can be found on the record's inner sleeve.

The band used two studios in Melbourne's Metropolis Studios. In one was Cave amongst his piles of paper, composing and recording; in the other, Harvey and Cohen working on the mixes. The sessions were efficient, and the atmosphere inspired confidence in everyone present. It was a happy environment – friends often visiting to witness the ongoing album construction, and little did they know they'd spontaneously end up contributing backing vocals at Cave's request.

On its April 1994 release, *Let Love In* proved to be the band's biggest triumph ever, and for good reason. *Henry's Dream* showcased raw, powerful 'trash-can' songs driven by acoustic guitar, but the arrangements here are more dense and expansive, making the songs sound cinematic: timpani, bells and all. The ugly, deranged sound of their roots is captured here, combined with an eclectic mix of genres, including funk and soul. Furthermore, the Hammond organ features more prominently, overall laying down a gothic backdrop for Cave's brooding and personal lyrics. One must only look at the album cover – which frames Cave looking up to the heavens in a backdrop of lurid bloody red – to get a sense of the album's gothic voodooism. It was arguably the band's most realised work to date, encompassing everything old and new that was theirs whilst setting up their future direction.

'Do You Love Me?' (Cave, Casey) (5:56)

This song and its album-closer sibling 'Do You Love Me? (Part 2)' were among the first to be recorded. Straight away, we're immersed in the album's cinematic world. With Casey's bass providing a bedrock, a wave of intermingling sounds washes over. The Hammond organ asserts its dominance, jittering guitar moves between the left and right channels, a crunchy guitar economically interjects, and a most entrancing descending melody is heard on the piano. Amongst this tense musical kaleidoscope, Cave details a narrator's inner torment caused by a volatile relationship with a woman who has 'God and all his devils inside her'. She offers 'a heart full of love' and 'a mind full of tyranny and terror' – the distress of such opposites leaving the narrator helpless as he eventually loses his grip on the relationship. There seems to be a suggestion of mental illness in the line 'Crazy bracelets around her wrists and her ankles' which could be a reference to hospital bands. The tension release comes in the chorus, which asks the question so pivotal to the narrator's torment – 'Do you love me?' – the chain-gang vocals are delivered with a violent aggression as if the narrator is releasing his pent-up frustration as he fails to find an answer to his question.

This track is an opener of a different calibre to 'Papa Won't Leave You, Henry' or 'Tupelo', but is still just as powerful.

'Nobody's Baby Now' (Cave) (3:52)
Another famous Cave ballad driven by melodic piano, its simplicity is a trademark of most of his love songs. The song was written for Johnny Cash, but Cave decided to keep it for himself. He sticks with convention, as the loss of a lover haunts the narrator, who's left questioning how one is meant to behave in the aftermath of such loss: 'I've read the poets and the analysts/Searched through the books on human behaviour'. Cave takes pride in the first verse, which 'takes so long to get to the point' he says. Indeed, before the lost lover is even introduced, we get a whole verse that parallels human behaviour with the 'mystery of Jesus Christ the Saviour'. Much like the idea of an enigmatic Jesus figure, there is no human reaction that can be regarded as definitive in the throes of loss – everybody reacts differently; therefore, human behaviour cannot be defined. For such a straightforward love song, there are stimulating and thought-provoking ideas.

'Loverman' (Cave) (6:21)
Covered by both Metallica and Depeche Mode's Martin Gore, this song combines sparse textures in the soul-inflected verses with moments of thrashing noise in the chorus – that almost hearkens back to the early post-Birthday-Party Bad Seeds sound of their debut. Even the quieter verses have subtle details so barely audible that an impression of sparsity is given when in reality, there are splashes of piano, guitar scratches and triangle hits alongside the more obvious bass, drums, bells and vocals. Cave initially had reservations when recording the song at Townhouse III, but these qualms were resolved once he added two spoken passages in which the loverman's lustful desires are spelt out just after the thrashing choruses. The doom-laden accompaniment to the character's animalistic and careless sexual hunger, makes for a chilling listening experience.

'Jangling Jack' (Cave) (2:47)

Here we encounter the character Jangling Jack – a naïve Englishman who's oblivious to the violent world of New York that he enters – one of the few times on the album where Cave relies on a character to voice his opinion. In a bar, Jack raises a toast to 'The losers and the winners/The good guys and the sinners', before being shot by someone who obviously disagrees. Through Jack's death sequence, we see the America that Cave sees and detests: 'Sees the berserk city/Sees the dead stacked in piles'. This aggressive track was composed in a day, the idea being to contrast the other more-cinematic tracks with something more abrasive and rock 'n' roll. Again, the punk sensibility reminds me of The Birthday Party, and while it's certainly not the strongest track – rather a frantic throwaway – it does add another flavour.

'Red Right Hand' (Cave, Harvey, Wydler) (6:10)

This is arguably the most famous Nick Cave song, having been popularised by its inclusion in four films of the *Scream* saga, and most recently as the main theme for the TV series *Peaky Blinders*. It's the album's centrepiece and has been a mainstay in the Bad Seeds' setlists. From that initial bell-tolling, it can be recognised as one of the band's most idiosyncratic moments. Here the Bad Seeds fuse a swampy funk-like riff with a 12-bar blues; its eerie tension a result of its sparsity. It's no wonder this works so well as a horror soundtrack, with the gothic bell-tolling, thunderous timpani hits and organ-drenched minor chords later down the line adding to the overall menace of the character who's depicted as this frightening, omniscient, all-powerful figure. A meandering oscillator eventually finds its way into the track, only adding to the mystery of this 'tall handsome man/In a dusty black coat with a red right hand'.

The song title was taken from John Milton's *Paradise Lost* and refers to the divine wrath of God; the demon Belial refers to the red right hand of God, which will wrathfully strike the Devil. But it seems unlikely that this figure is God. In fact, his identity remains enigmatic as Cave keeps us guessing, 'He's a ghost, he's a god, he's a man, he's a guru'. The industrial landscape outlined could house a number of people; perhaps a drug dealer or maybe a corrupt politician – both figures that are worshipped by helpless individuals who represent the 'one microscopic cog in his catastrophic plan/Designed and directed by his red right hand'. The meaning is unclear, but the writing provides a fertile breeding ground for many interpretations. Given its profundity, it's no wonder Cave rejected the track's use for a tampon advertisement.

'I Let Love In' (Cave) (4:14)

The trials and tribulations of love are again explored through some of the most beautiful lines, including the opening 'Despair and Deception/Love's ugly little twins' – emotions that are characterised and come knocking at the door in tow with love and the final crushing line 'Far worse to be Love's lover than the lover that Love has scorned': what a line! The song title gives a false impression of love being something energising and joy-provoking when let in, but the dark truth is that love can also be something incredibly damaging: 'Never has my tormentor come in such a cunning disguise'. And so, the repeated line 'I let love in' is the opposite of what we expect: regretful rather than uplifting. Framing this heart-wrenching truth about love is a country-inflected ballad propelled by a beautiful guitar melody and accompanying piano and acoustic guitar.

'Thirsty Dog' (Cave) (3:48)

This is the album's second throwaway thrashing-punk track, composed to add an aggressive energy, yet arguably it's Cave's most personal song. It's not that hard to fathom as he profusely apologises to his lover for his self-destructive lifestyle. It's likely that the song most explicitly documents the disintegrating relationship between Cave and Carneiro, alcohol playing a key role: 'I'm sorry that I'm always pissed/I'm sorry that I exist'. There are melodramatic moments, such as when Cave likens the relationship to some sort of battleground: 'I'm sorry for this three-year war/For the setting up of camps and wire and trenches'. However, back in reality, Cave can be found in his usual watering hole The Thirsty Dog, to miserably quench that thirst and continue the self-loathing.

'Ain't Gonna Rain Anymore' (Cave) (3:46)

With lost love being the flavour of the day, we are presented with another slow track exploring the theme, the lyrics for which were written in the studio with help from friends and band members. The girl in question is representative of a storm that 'blew to pieces my snug little world'. But now she's gone, the narrator is 'Left to drift on a dead calm sea', and, to his dismay, 'There is no sign of rain'. The strings take centre stage here, emphasising the chorus's emotional despair with long sustained notes whilst a more-stuttered delivery in the verse creates a moodiness. The mood is incredibly dreary and glum, but it's a moving listen. Interestingly, Warren Ellis of Australian instrumental rock band Dirty Three (much later Cave's second-in-command) makes his debut with the Bad Seeds on violin here and on the closing track.

'Lay Me Low' (Cave) (5:08)

Both humorous and at times more serious, Cave self-mockingly reads his own obituary to this funeral dirge. Never has the organ sounded so holy as on this track, with the choir of the Bad Seeds adding soul inflections. Of the more amusing lines in Cave's obituary, there is his old teacher saying Cave was 'one of God's sorrier creatures', and the natural events in the wake of Cave's death ('The sea will rage, the sky will storm/All man and beast will mourn') appear very melodramatic, but the thought of it is rather gratifying. But then, there are more-realistic lines, like 'My friends will give up the fight/They'll see my work in a different light', in which Cave identifies the tendency for opinions of an individual to change once they've died.

'Do You Love Me? (Part Two)' (Cave) (6:12)

If its sibling track which opened the album, asked the pivotal question as a consequence of a volatile relationship – probably due to mental illness – the question arises out of something completely different and more harrowing here. This is similar to the opener, albeit a lot more ambient and ghostly. The crunchy guitars remain, but a mellow and mournful Rhodes replaces the Hammond organ. Warren Ellis' painful violin melody is superb upon its entrance in the second verse, with further string parts added with each new verse, intermingling in a pool of ethereal sorrow and pain. By the final verse, the opening track's piano melody is fully realised and can be heard clearly on the lines 'Do you love me?/I love you handsome'. As to who is asking the question and why they are asking it, the reasons are unnerving – our narrator is a young boy who is sexually abused by a paedophile with 'girlish eyes' in a cinema, and consequently, this first experience dictates the rest of his life. The parallel between the paedophile and the ape on the screen highlights the animalistic and barbaric acts being committed by this man – not just physically, but on the boy's future mental well-being: 'The clock of my boyhood was wound down and stopped'. And so the pivotal question is now being asked by the victim of molestation: groomed to do so. I suppose the paedophile could also be asking the question; both possibilities are equally grim. There's a lot more to unpack here, but overall this is some of Cave's bravest songwriting, and an excellent closing track despite the discomfort it arouses.

Murder Ballads (1996)

Personnel:
Nick Cave: vocals, piano, organ, Hammond organ, gunshots, string arrangement
Mick Harvey: drums, guitar, acoustic guitar, organ, wind organ, backing vocals, string arrangement, bass, Hammond organ, space belt, percussion
Blixa Bargeld: guitar, screams, vocals
Martyn P. Casey: bass
Conway Savage: piano, backing vocals, organ
Jim Sclavunos: drums, percussion, bells, tambourine
Thomas Wydler: drums, tambourine, maracas, vocals
Guest musicians:
PJ Harvey: vocals ('Henry Lee', 'Death Is Not The End')
Terry Edwards: horns ('Lovely Creature')
Katharine Blake: additional vocals ('Lovely Creature')
Kylie Minogue: vocals ('Where The Wild Roses Grow', 'Death Is Not The End')
Jen Anderson, Sue Simpson: violin ('Where The Wild Roses Grow')
Kerran Coulter: viola ('Where The Wild Roses Grow')
Helen Mountfort: cello ('Where the Wild Roses Grow')
Hugo Race: guitar ('The Curse Of Millhaven')
Warren Ellis: violin, accordion ('The Curse Of Millhaven')
Marielle Del Conte: additional vocals ('The Kindness Of Strangers')
Anita Lane: crying ('The Kindness of Strangers'); vocals ('Death Is Not The End')
Geraldine Johnston, Liz Corcoran: additional vocals ('Crow Jane')
Shane Macgowan: vocals ('Death Is Not The End')
Brian Hooper: bass ('Death Is Not The End')
The Moron Tabernacle Choir: 'The Curse Of Millhaven'
Recorded at Atlantis, Sing Sing and Metropolis Studios, Melbourne; Wessex Studios, London, 1993-1995
Producers: Tony Cohen, Victor Van Vugt, The Bad Seeds
Label: Mute Records
Release date: 5 February 1996
Chart positions: UK: 8, USA: -, Australia: 3
Running time: 58:43

After the recording and release of *Love Let In*, Cave's most revealing record to date – which Cave described as 'a very personal, painful record to write' in a 1996 *Alternative Press* interview – he needed a break from writing himself into his art: 'I really didn't want to have anything more to do with my problems, examining my problems'. At the end of the *Let Love In* mixing sessions, two songs had been written, which would form the basis of Cave's next project. One was a sprawling 30-verse piano epic titled 'O'Malley's Bar'. The other had the working title 'Red Right Hand II', which would later become 'Song Of Joy' – the opening track to an album of murder ballads: a venture Cave had always wanted to pursue. Indeed, it was no secret that Cave had a fascination with the subject of killing – murder crops up everywhere in his back catalogue, such as in 'John Finn's Wife' and 'Up Jumped The Devil'. So it seems rather ironic that only at this moment – presented with two new lengthy compositions that were deemed too dark for *Let Love In* – the band decided to dedicate an entire album to the subject.

When the word 'ballad' is used in this context, it doesn't refer to what one might associate with Cave. Tracks like 'Nobody's Baby Now' and 'The Ship Song' can be conceived as love ballads. But in this new context, the word 'ballad' refers to an exceedingly old narrative tradition in which sensationalism champions over historical accuracy. The origins of the murder ballad date back to medieval times, when people would orally recite local legends and crimes of passion. Over time, these tales would eventually be put to paper and given a musical backdrop, and they continued to be popular in England until the 19th century. Therefore, there are many different readings of the same murder ballads. Cave reinterpreted some of these traditional murder ballads, and also composed some of his own.

Unlike the previous few records – for which the groundwork for each composition had been laid with demos and rehearsals – the sessions for *Murder Ballads* were much looser, and songs would be composed and recorded live one after another at an astonishing rate. Cave considered this to be a 'novelty album' – an extracurricular activity providing him with some light relief from the personal outpourings on *Let Love In*. Therefore the loose approach to the proceedings injected a sense of fun – further emphasised by the incredible number of guest musicians. This was an open, exploratory and malleable project that embraced a communal aspect, and in doing so, created an enjoyable atmosphere. Little did Cave know that the presence of one guest, in particular, would gift the record with immeasurable commercial success upon its release: to his surprise and dismay.

The *Murder Ballads* album wasn't composed for the same audience that discovered Cave through the entrancing *Let Love In* album, but rather was to separate the wheat from the chaff as explained in the same 1996 *Alternative Press* interview: 'I don't want to be very popular, so we tried to make a record which would turn a lot of people off us. I wanted to make an extremely difficult record. I thought it *was* an extremely difficult record. Obviously, I have no fucking idea'. Despite the album's horrific innards, which boast a body count of 64 – surely enough to shock and offend Cave's audience – it overtook *Let Love In* as the band's most commercially successful album to that point, selling over 1,000,000 copies. Cave underestimated the power of having commercial queen Kylie Minogue as a guest on the album – her involvement (which led to an appearance for Cave on *Top of the Pops*) contributing to the album's success. But it would be wrong to attribute this success entirely to Kylie's involvement. *Murder Ballads* is an outstanding piece of work that's unique in the Cave catalogue – an album that resurrects an old tradition and injects a whole new sense of horror and profanity into these old murder ballads. The album acted as the perfect transition between *Let Love In* and the highly regarded *The Boatman's Call*, which saw Cave return to a state of self-examination in the throes of heartbreak.

'Song Of Joy' (Cave) (6:47)

This was one of the two songs composed during the *Let Love In* sessions that gave Cave the idea to record an album of murder ballads. The song title is ironic, considering the song is devoid of any such thing. Gloomy, eerie and spectral, the pulsing one-note heart-monitor-like sound and suspenseful repetitive drum pattern make for a chilling soundscape for the gruesome story. The oral tradition of the murder ballad is made clear as the narrator addresses the ballad to an anonymous listener, from whom he pleads for sympathy. He goes into the nitty-gritty of the murder of his wife Joy and their three children:

> Joy had been bound with electrical tape
> In her mouth a gag
> She'd been stabbed repeatedly
> And stuffed into a sleeping bag

It's no wonder Cave failed to see the album's potential popularity with such vivid and upsetting murder descriptions. This murderous act is made even more creepy through the writing the killer leaves on the wall in the family's blood. It reads 'Red right hand', which explains why the song took the working title of 'Red Right Hand II'. The common theory is that the narrator is the murderer in question and is about to enter the listener's house and leave his distinctive mark. Alternatively, one might suggest the murderer is, in fact, the *listener*, and the narrator is the one about to meet his maker.

'Stagger Lee' (Trad., Cave) (5:15)

Without a doubt, this is the most foul-mouthed Bad Seeds track in existence. In a tale of utter debauchery, the swaggering Stagger Lee enters a bar, and after a less-than-civil exchange with the bartender, 'Stag put four holes in his motherfucking head'. He then has a dalliance with a prostitute named Nellie Brown, who says that Stag must be gone before her man Billy Dilly arrives. Having asserted that he'd 'crawl over 50 good pussies just to get to one fat boy's asshole', Stag waits for Billy Dilly, who, upon his arrival, fellates Stag in fear of Stag's death threat, before Stag inevitably shoots him anyway.

It is interesting that this is one of the most popular songs on the album and indeed an overall fan favourite when this was one of the final tracks to be composed just as the album was deemed finished. Inspiration for recording the song came from Bad Seeds drummer Jim Sclavunos showing Cave a book which included the traditional ballad. Having added a few touches of his own, Cave's version was uglier and exposed a heightened depravity. When it came to adding music, it was Casey's iconic bass part that set the wheels in motion for the completion of a charged accompaniment. Blues and folk are absent, replaced with Cave's gangster-rap delivery, all captured on the second take.

'Henry Lee' (Trad., Cave) (3:58)

For the first duet of the album, Cave shares the mic with British recording artist PJ Harvey, in a meditative and melancholy retelling of the traditional folk ballad 'Young Hunting'. If you listen to this album's 'The Curse Of Millhaven', you'll notice that 'Henry Lee' is a slower and sweeter version of its frenzied charge, characterised by a docile lilt and graceful melody. The accompanying video is similarly romantic, showing Cave and PJ Harvey teasing each other in a scene of passionate intimacy, which is no surprise given they'd become romantically involved at around the time of the album's making. However, this is deception at its finest, as such innocence masks the horror of the tale lurking beneath. Quite simply, the character of Henry Lee is stabbed to death by the girl he rejects, his body unceremoniously dumped down a well for nobody to find. It's difficult to reconcile the revolting image of his corpse wasting away, with the innocent little bird that perches on his body. The discomfort such a combination arouses heightens the horror here.

'Lovely Creature' (Bargeld, Casey, Cave, Harvey, Wydler) (4:13)

A whirlwind of ambient background noise, jittering Hammond organ, sharp guitar stabs and persistent snare rolls contribute to this haunting track shrouded in mist and mystery. The 'lovely creature' the narrator describes is innocent and delicate, her 'hair full of ribbons/And green gloves on her hands', heightened further by the equally innocent and playful 'la la' refrain: altogether contrasting with the harsh landscape communicated musically and lyrically. We know that she agrees to walk with the narrator – 'A joyful man she led' – and we also learn that the narrator returns home alone and the girl's body is left 'beneath the slow drifting sands' of the desert. It's likely that, in an act of madness, the narrator murdered the girl, which is suggested in the threatening line 'At night the deserts writhed with diabolical things'. But the method of killing and the motivation behind it, remain enigmatic.

'Where The Wild Roses Grow' (Cave) (3:57)

The album's second duet features the odd and unlikely combination of Cave and pop star Kylie Minogue, that nonetheless rewarded Cave with his biggest UK hit single and even an appearance on *Top of the Pops,* which Cave fondly speaks of in a 2005 issue of *The Weekend Australian:*

> Yeah. I was on *Top of the Pops* two weeks running with Kylie, trying to fumble my way through the song. And then I remember being in a toy shop getting a toy for my son and this little kid coming up to me in a Power Rangers outfit, and he goes, 'Are you that old guy that was on with Kylie Minogue the other night?'. He was just this little kid, but he really loved the song. And I'm just

like, 'Oh, fuck off you little bastard'. But it suddenly occurred to me that these people may even be buying the record, and it deeply troubled me.

Given that Kylie's character becomes the victim of a brutal murder involving her head being smashed in with a rock at the hand of Cave's character, it's remarkable that such an explicit song found its way onto *Top of the Pops*. But it was probably wholly the music rather than the story that grasped the viewers, as, like on 'Henry Lee', the gruesome story is overshadowed by the romantic allure of the acoustic guitar and aching strings that deceptively give the impression of a straightforward love ballad. But it's more complicated than that – there is undoubtedly a romance between these two characters, but the love that Cave's character exhibits is twisted, driven only by the female character's innocence. Once he's robbed her of that innocence, he also steals her life, and Kylie's character recounts these events from a sort-of afterlife. Anyone unfamiliar with Cave's work who bought the record on the strength of this single *must* have been alienated by the rest of the album, which is saturated in explicit gruesomeness.

'The Curse Of Millhaven' (Cave) (6:55)

This is the original faster version of 'Henry Lee' that sounds like a jovial sing-along hoedown straight out of a tavern, complete with accordion courtesy of Warren Ellis. No less than 20 children, among other citizens of the town of Millhaven, become the victims of the sadistic 15-year-old Loretta. In the course of the song, she proudly admits to each and every one of her killings, though she refutes the accusation that she killed Professor O'Rye's dog, Biko. This is perhaps the first example of the album's black humour. Yes, the crimes she admits to are savage, but some of her lines provoke laughter – such as 'Foul play can really get a small town going' and 'They asked me if I feel remorse and I answer, 'Why of course!/There's so much more I could've done if they'd let me''. It's silly, it's playful, and it's not to be taken too seriously.

'The Kindness Of Strangers' (Cave) (4:39)

This is a rather sorrowful piano-led ode to the character Mary Bellows who is murdered at the hands of a stranger she meets on the road of discovery away from her miserable Arkansas home. It opens boldly with the image of Bellows 'cuffed to the bed/With a rag in her mouth and a bullet in her head', before detailing how she wound up dead. Richard Slade meets her on her travels to find 'the deep blue sea', and once she has accomplished this, he accompanies her to a 'cheap little place' to stay, before Mary initially turns him away at the door. Letting him back in proves to be a significant mistake, but we are told nothing more, and the opening line is merely repeated, as Anita Lane's crying can be heard in the background; the track closing with a warning for mothers to keep their daughters at home and to teach them to 'shun the company of strangers'. But it's been suggested that Slade's killing of Mary was an act of kindness, hence the song title. After accomplishing what she set out to do, Mary would've been forced to go back to her miserable life. So when she let Slade back into the room out of 'hope and loneliness', perhaps she welcomed her death.

'Crow Jane' (Casey, Cave) (4:14)

A further 20 people lose their lives at the hands of Crow Jane, who has 'horrors in her head that her tongue dare not name'. The astute Cave fan will recognise this name from *And the Ass Saw the Angel*, as it's a nickname given to Euchrid's drunken mother, Jane Crowley. The character first appeared in the lyric of an early version of the song originally meant for *The Firstborn Is Dead*, but it never came to fruition, so her character was instead used for the book. It's certainly no surprise that the song was written at the time of the second album – its gutter blues wouldn't sound out of place on that record. The Crow Jane here is not too dissimilar to the one in the book: both appearing to enjoy the booze. Unfortunately for the Crow Jane in *this* song, her whisky is stolen by 20 miners who also take turns raping her before returning to a place called New Haven. In retaliation, Crow Jane buys some guns, travels to New Haven, kills all 20 miners and returns home 'laughing all the way back from the new town'.

'O'Malley's Bar' (Cave) (14:28)

Similar to 'The Curse Of Millhaven' in its leaning towards black humour, the album's biggest killing spree occurs here – at an endurance-testing 15 minutes, such a high death count is no surprise. Framed by a loose accompaniment that sees piano and Hammond organ stabbing away over a grounded bass line, the swaggering narrator (who oddly resembles Cave with his 'enviable height' and handsome exterior 'from a certain angle and in a certain light') embarks on the most farcical conquest as he enters O'Malley's bar and gleefully shoots the place up. We are given names and details of each character, and then he specifies the method of killing, whether that be a bullet to the head, stomach or chest, strangulation, or – in the case of Jerry Bellows (interesting name) – an ashtray to the head. Again, the comedy is prevalent. The way O'Malley's wife's head lands 'in the sink with all the dirty dishes' after being shot, may provoke a giggle. And perhaps the self-imposed graceful heroism of the narrator – with his 'hair combed back like a raven's wing' and 'muscles hard and tight' – might also bring a chuckle. With everyone dead and only one bullet left, the narrator has the option to kill himself in order to avoid being taken away by the police surrounding the bar. But in the end, he decides a life in prison is far better than death – contradicting his previous murder spree justification: that he had no free will. As they drive him away from the barbaric scene, he begins a head count, and if I'm right, the total stands at 12.

'Death Is Not The End' (Bob Dylan) (4:26)

As the only song here that doesn't involve a murder, Cave's Dylan cover aims to end the album on an uplifting note for those feeling despondent from everything that's come before. A multitude of singers take a turn at the mic here. In addition to the return of PJ Harvey and Kylie Minogue, we have The Pogues' Shane MacGowan, Anita Lane and Bad Seeds members Bargeld and Wydler. A chorus that has them all singing together communicates the hopeful message that despite all the murder that's taken place, death is not the end. Granted, it does sound like a whimsical tune a group of drunken individuals would bellow near closing time at the pub: insincere, a little jokey, but elevating nonetheless.

The Boatman's Call (1997)

Personnel:
Nick Cave: vocals, piano, organ, Casio keyboard, vibes, keyboard
Mick Harvey: electric and acoustic guitars, bass, organ, vibes, bass organ, backing vocals, xylophone
Blixa Bargeld: guitar, piano treatment, backing vocals
Martyn P. Casey: bass, backing vocals
Warren Ellis: violin, accordion, piano, looped violin
Conway Savage: piano, backing vocals
Jim Sclavunos: drums, melodica, bells, percussion, organ, bongos, tambourine
Thomas Wydler: drums, maraca, backing vocals
Producers: Flood, The Bad Seeds
Recorded at Sarm West Studios, London, June-August 1996
Label: Mute Records
Release date: 3 March 1997
Chart positions: UK: 22, USA: 155, Australia: 5
Running Time: 52:07

After witnessing the gruesome crimes of passion detailed on the horrifying *Murder Ballads* album, I don't think any Cave fan could've predicted the direction the next Bad Seeds album would take. *Murder Ballads* – with the grisly themes the group had always ruminated on – brought an end to this period, and the Bad Seeds would never sound the same again as explained by Mick Harvey in a 2009 *Record Collector* interview:

> The *Murder Ballads* album is a kind of punctuation mark for that whole era which we'd completed with *Let Love In* – which, in a way, perfected what we were trying to do with the Bad Seeds. It was like a freewheeling open kind of project, which still embodies the same kinds of musical things, then opened up this weird thing for Nick to enter, which was much more highly personalised.

Indeed the band's dynamic would be tested in the making of *The Boatman's Call,* which saw Cave return to a personal writing style that went even deeper than the personal themes on *Let Love In*: Cave explains in issue #132 of *The Red Hand Files* that '*The Boatman's Call* was a record born of personal misfortune that led to a departure from fictitious narrative songwriting, into a kind of writing that was more autobiographical'. The recent upheavals of Cave being back in the throes of heroin addiction and battling his feelings following the dissolution of his short-lived affair with PJ Harvey formed the basis of the new record.

Cave took full musical control of the album, choosing to abandon the full band setup so fundamental to earlier Bad Seeds albums. Instead, Cave wanted to frame his autobiographical musings with piano-driven songs that would otherwise be instrumentally sparse. Mick Harvey – who'd always been a sort of advisor and creative second-in-command – was forced to take a back seat, as was the other longtime Bad Seeds member Blixa Bargeld, whose economical guitar-playing somehow had to become even more economical. Overall, the band were instructed to embellish as little as possible so Cave could rely solely on his own abilities as a pianist, vocalist and lyricist to communicate his vulnerable emotions. The band's ability to adapt and restrain themselves is a testament to their professionalism, as Cave detailed in issue #57 of *The Red Hand Files*: 'The Bad Seeds, to their eternal credit, stepped back and just let these piano-driven songs be. There are few bands on Earth that understand that to *not* play, can be as important as its opposite'.

In 1996 – the year before the album's release – Cave recorded *The Flesh Made Word*: a lecture for BBC Radio 3's religious services, describing his relationship with God and the Bible. In 1998, Cave wrote a lecture for the Vienna Poetry Festival – titled *The Secret Life of the Love Song* – in which he delved into the nuances of the love song, using his own as points of insight. The themes of religion and love converge to the greatest effect on *The Boatman's Call*; the devastation and pain caused by the breakdown of Cave's relationship with Harvey, works in tandem with his problematic relationship with God. It's often tricky to fathom Cave's religious position, but the wisdom he imparts in his lectures goes some way towards explaining the meaning of the divine undercurrents that run through the album. In *The Flesh Made Word*, he asks the question, 'Why do we need the church to bring us close to God when he already lives within us?'. Cave appears to construct his own theology separate from institutional religion, in which he suggests there's a God that exists within every individual. In *The Secret Life of the Love Song,* Cave asserts, 'The actualisation of God through the medium of the love song, remains my primary motivation as an artist'. I believe it's through the love songs on *The Boatman's Call* that Cave is able to actualise his own theology and connect with his inner God. The female presence Cave addresses could easily represent this inner God and also PJ Harvey.

On release, *The Boatman's Call* received unanimous critical acclaim, and many heralded it as his best album to date. *Melody Maker*'s Jennifer Nine described the album as 'The most astonishingly, fearlessly gentle record of his long and brilliant career', whilst James McNair of *Mojo* described it as 'sparse, stark and unrelentingly honest', believing it seemed 'likely to become the career milestone for Cave'. He was right – even in 2022, it remains Cave's magnum opus. Although, recent Bad Seeds albums like *Skeleton Tree* and *Ghosteen* – which inherited their similar autobiographical writing from *The Boatman's Call* – could easily rival that album's legendary status.

Contrary to the universal positivity surrounding the album on its release, Cave typically belittled his ultra-personal offering, calling it 'a big heroic melodrama out of a bog-standard rejection'. Nowadays, he's a little warmer towards his introspective masterpiece. It would be hard for the band to top the

Above: The first stable Bad Seeds lineup conceived during the time of *Henry's Dream* in the early 90s.

Above: A shot of the band including members – from left to right – Ellis, Cave, Casey and Sclavunos in approximately 2017.

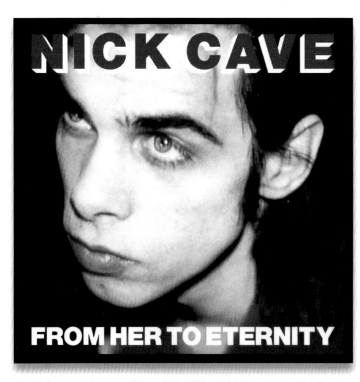

Left: Cave looks as deranged as the many characters present on *From Her to Eternity*. The album credits the photograph on the front to Marina whilst the polaroids on the back were taken by Jessamy Calkin, the band's manager for a time. (*Mute*)

Right: The black and white photograph of Cave taken by Jutta Heinglein effectively encapsulates the moody blues present on *The Firstborn is Dead*. (*Mute*)

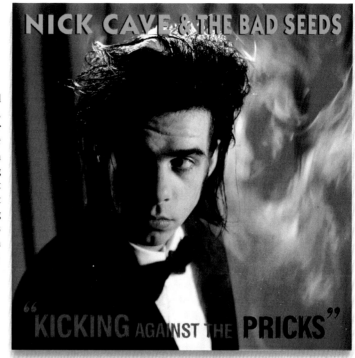

Right: Captured by Peter Milne, the artwork for *Kicking Against the Pricks* sees an immaculate-looking Cave refining his art as a composer. It was initially going to be a double LP as 23 tracks had been recorded. (*Mute*)

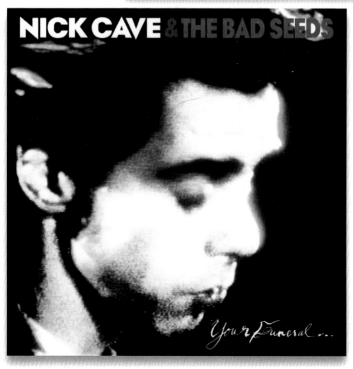

Left: As well as this image used for the *Your Funeral* EP, there was a mirror image of Cave with his eyes wide open used for the *My Trial* EP. (*Mute*)

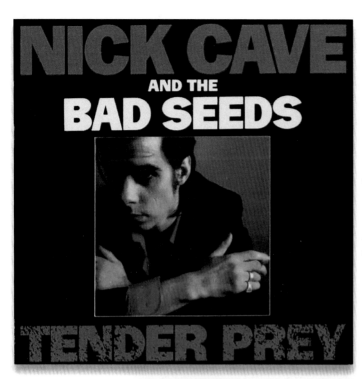

Left: Included with the first 5,000 vinyl copies of *Tender Prey* was a 12-inch disc of Cave narrating extracts from his first novel *And the Ass Saw the Angel*. (*Mute*)

Right: Some of the initial vinyl copies of *The Good Son* came with a 7-inch disc of acoustic versions of tracks from *Tender Prey,* later released on the *B-sides & Rarities* record in 2005. (*Mute*)

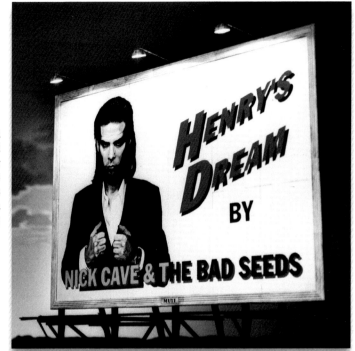

Right: Anton Corbijn's billboard design for *Henry's Dream* advertises the snarl of Cave's acoustic favela punk. (*Mute*)

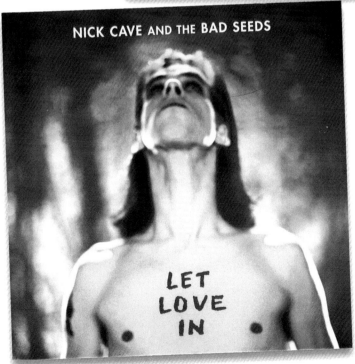

Left: The artwork for *Let Love In* is a technicolour delight that manages to appear both horrifying yet elegant. (*Mute*)

Left: The romantic music video for 'Henry Lee' from *Murder Ballads* perfectly captured the chemistry between Cave and guest star PJ Harvey.

Right: In contrast, Cave here looks menacing (despite the pink T-shirt) in this very wild and energetic video for the foul-mouthed 'Stagger Lee' from *Murder Ballads*.

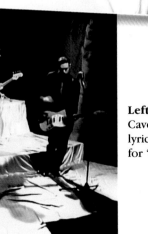

Left: The scene in which Cave delivers his sweary lyrics in the music video for 'Stagger Lee'.

Right: Cave looking murderous in the music video for 'Where the Wild Roses Grow' from *Murder Ballads.*

Left: Guest star Kylie Minogue plays the victim in the music video for 'Where the Wild Roses Grow'.

Right: In 2014, Cave and Kylie performed 'Where the Wild Roses Grow' live at Koko in London for the *20,000 Days on Earth* documentary film. (*Ian Forsyth and Jane Pollard*)

Left: Swiss painter Jean-Frederic Shnyder was instructed by Cave not to include any horror clichés on the *Murder Ballads* cover. The result was a painting that looks like something from a fairy-tale, albeit a chilling one. (*Mute*)

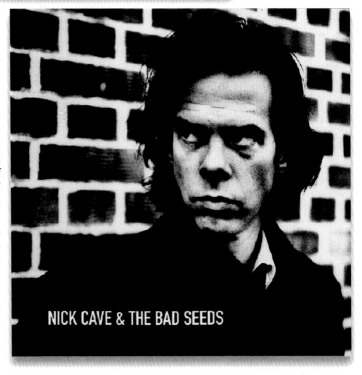

Right: The black and white photograph of Cave against the brick wall for the cover of *The Boatman's Call* was taken by Anton Corbijn, a perfect visual aid to Cave's mourning of love. (*Mute*)

Right: Tony Clark's painting for the cover of *No More Shall We Part* visually captures the subdued melancholy of the album. (*Mute*)

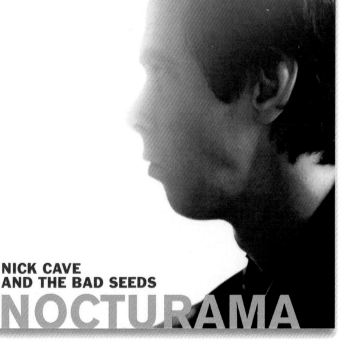

Left: The *Nocturama* album cover is not the most striking – a good visual indicator of the music on the album. (*Mute*)

Left: Cave's questionable moustache up close in this *Dig, Lazarus, Dig!!!* interview.

Right: Riding on the success of *Dig, Lazarus, Dig!!!*, the band performed songs from their latest album along with beloved classics in this BBC Four session in 2008.

Left: Another still from the same BBC Four session.

Right: Cave performing 'I Need You' from *Skeleton Tree*'s companion film *One More Time with Feeling.* (*Andrew Dominik*)

Left: Warren Ellis adds warm lashes of synth for the track 'I Need You' from *Skeleton Tree*'s companion film *One More Time with Feeling.* (*Andrew Dominik*)

Right: Martyn P. Casey on bass performing 'I Need You' from *Skeleton Tree*'s companion film *One More Time with Feeling.* (*Andrew Dominik*)

Nick Cave
& The Bad Seeds
Abattoir Blues / The Lyre of Orpheus

Left: The physical packages for *Abattoir/Lyre* were perhaps the band's most regal – perfect for a grandiose comeback double album. (*Mute*)

Right: The dazzling light sculpture on the *Dig, Lazarus, Dig!!!* cover was created by Tim Noble & Sue Webster. (*Mute*)

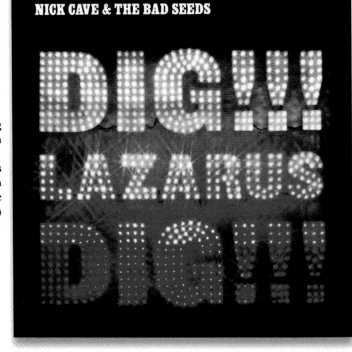

Right: Dominique Isserman's photograph for the cover of *Push the Sky Away* spontaneously captured Cave's naked wife illuminated by the light streaming in from behind. (*Bad Seed Ltd*)

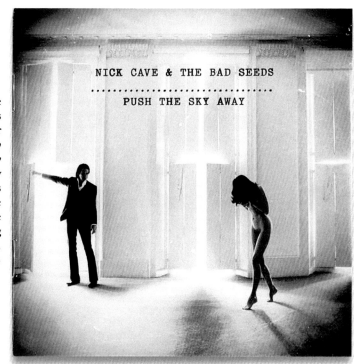

Left: The minimalist design of the *Skeleton Tree* album cover mirrors the themes within the music and was created by the Hingston Studio in London. (*Bad Seed Ltd*)

Left: A full band shot of The Bad Seeds performing at Glastonbury in 2013.

Right: Cave certainly enjoys getting up close and personal at his gigs as exemplified here at Glastonbury in 2013.

Left: George Vjestica on acoustic guitar duties for the 2017 Royal Arena show in Copenhagen, released later as *Distant Sky: Live in Copenhagen*. (*David Barnard*)

Right: From left to right, Larry Mullins, Jim Sclavunos and Martyn P. Casey performing at the 2017 *Distant Sky* show in Copenhagen. (*David Barnard*)

Left: A full band shot captured at the 2017 *Distant Sky* show in Copenhagen. (*David Barnard*)

Right: Warren Ellis performing at the 2017 *Distant Sky* show in Copenhagen. (*David Barnard*)

Left: First revealed in issue #63 of *The Red Hand Files* before the album's release, the *Ghosteen* artwork pictures the 'hopeful and jubilant beyond' that he and his listeners journey towards. (*Bad Seeds Ltd*)

Above: Cave performing 'Ghosteen Speaks' from *This Much I Know to Be True*. (*Andrew Dominik*)

success of *The Boatman's Call*: everything about the Bad Seeds – the sound, the dynamic and the way they cooperated – had changed forever.

'Into My Arms' (Cave) (4:15)

My first experience of Nick Cave began with those three ascending piano chords and the arresting opening lines, 'I don't believe in an interventionist God/But I know, Darling, that you do'. The scene is set from those lines alone, which instantly pair love with religious wrestling; these themes being further explored over a simple hymn-like piano accompaniment along with Casey's fluid bass part. Many commentators would probably agree that here Cave pleads with an interventionist God that he doesn't believe in, to watch over and protect his lost lover and perhaps even direct her back into his arms. I believe Cave is addressing the God from within, who happens to be female. He rejects the biblical notion of an 'interventionist God' and 'the existence of angels', instead asserting 'but I believe in love'. The certainty of love replaces the doubts presented by an interventionist God, and for Cave, institutional religion fails to bring him close to God. Whereas love – and more specifically, the love song – enables him to establish an intimacy with his inner God. The chorus calls for such spiritual intimacy in the repeated line 'Into my arms, O Lord'. Such spiritual yearning encapsulates the feeling of 'saudade' that Cave refers to in *The Secret Life of the Love Song*: 'An inexplicable longing; an unnamed and enigmatic yearning of the soul'. The vehicle of the love song fulfils this yearning, which brings Cave in intimate contact with his inner God. This track is my favourite Cave album opener, and I'm sure I'm not alone when I say it's my all-time favourite Cave song.

The track has been featured in over a dozen films and TV shows, while also being an unsurprising song choice at weddings. Cave performed the song at the funeral of INXS singer Michael Hutchence: who Cave was friendly with in his youth.

'Lime Tree Arbour' (Cave) (2:56)

There's more of a full band setup here, with the addition of drums and warbling Hammond organ, piano and bass. Religion takes a back seat as Cave's lover takes on the full responsibility of providing safety and protection in a harsh and unforgiving world:

There will always be suffering
It flows through life like water
I put my hand over hers
Down in the lime-tree arbour

But the lover Cave refers to becomes something closer to a superior force in the lines 'There is a hand that protects me/And I do love her so'. Therefore, I believe Cave is once again addressing his inner God: her presence resembling the illusionary shelter of the lime tree arbour.

'People Ain't No Good' (Cave) (5:42)

Piano, bass and drums are the staple here, with gentle vibes and aching violins entering later on when Cave makes funeral preparations for the death of love: 'To our love send a dozen white lilies/To our love send a coffin of wood'. He uses natural imagery to chart the decay of a marriage, beginning with the healthful image of 'cherry trees' raining blossoms down upon the newlyweds. Later on, these trees have been stripped of their blossom, leaving a bare tree in their place, 'shaking its fists in the air': this tree is now devoid of life and full of rage. And so, with the death of their marriage comes the death of their love, their inability to stay true to their vows exemplifying the message that 'People just ain't no good'. This is not a hateful assertion against humanity, but rather a cruel fact of life – even if in our hearts we're not bad, we are by default prone to unintentionally messing things up.

'Brompton Oratory' (Cave) (4:06)

Underscored by a mellow soundscape complete with drum samples, the divine makes an almighty return as Cave enters the 'great shadowed vault' of the Brompton Oratory Cathedral to witness a service. Cave explains the story behind the song in a 1997 *MOJO* interview:

> In the Brompton Oratory, I was thinking about a particular girl that had left me, and found that the church wasn't a lot of help ... When I go to church, I have to take so much of it as metaphor, and I find it very irritating. The sermons are often pathetic and untrue, based on terrible misrepresentations of the bible.

This obviously refers to PJ Harvey. But in my reading of it, the girl referred to is Cave's inner God, who becomes the subject of his thoughts during the service, and consequently, he takes part in an intimate holy communion with *her*, as opposed to Christ.

We start with a reading 'from Luke 24/Where Christ returned to his loved ones'. This is the album's only explicit reference to the New Testament, recounting Jesus' resurrection and the return to his followers, who are initially kept from recognising him. It's a fitting reading considering Cave is in a similar state of doubt regarding the identity of an institutional God: 'A beauty impossible to define/A beauty impossible to believe'. It's in this moment of scepticism that the act of communion unifies him with his inner God, rather than taking him closer to the institutional God he's meant to be directing his thoughts to: 'The smell of you still on my hands/As I bring the cup up to my lips'. Here we see a marriage of the sacred and the profane in which the drinking of the blood represents the exchanging of bodily fluids. In comparison with the opening track, there's a greater intimacy between Cave and his inner God here. The definitive rejection of orthodox religion in favour of his inner God, comes when he surmises 'No God up in the sky/No Devil beneath the sea/Could do the job that you did/Of bringing me to my knees'. Only his inner God can do that: a position of prayer, but one with sexual connotations. Once again – even in the worshipping place of institutional religion: the 'stone apostles' being a cold reminder of its unmalleable creed – the love song enables Cave to reignite the connection between himself and the God within.

'There Is A Kingdom' (Cave) (4:52)

This uplifting track has a fuller band setup that pairs acoustic guitar and piano to the sweetest effect. Hymnal undertones are once more exercised as Cave attempts to establish his own place in the world and the place of God: 'The starry heavens above me/The moral law within/So the world appears' – a dichotomy between Heaven, existing in the stars, and Earth, characterised by moral law. However, Cave's theology comes into play during the chorus: 'There is a kingdom/There is a king/And he lives without/And he lives within'. Cave rejects the idea that Heaven and Earth are separate, instead unifying the kingdom of Heaven with the self, suggesting God and Heaven can be accessed from within.

'(Are You) The One That I've Been Waiting For?' (Cave) (4:05)

This is another full band track, but if the previous few have been, to a certain extent, uplifting, the false fantasies of love are here pushed aside to let in a harsh reality. A great anticipation builds in the first three verses, where Cave can feel his one true love moving towards him, entrusting the feelings provoked by his heart and soul: that 'All will be revealed'. But a musical change in verse four disrupts this anticipation as Cave delivers the pivotal lines:

O we will know, won't we?
The stars will explode in the sky
O but they don't, do they?
Stars have their moment and then they die

The image of the stars and their existence communicates the pain of not knowing. On Earth, we are able to see the stars due to the light they emit, but whether they're alive or dead is uncertain. Stars do not 'explode' in order to announce their life or death, but they have their 'moment', almost going unnoticed. Love is just as fleeting and mysterious, refusing to provide Cave with the earth-shattering revelation he yearns for.

The final verse returns to the previous musical format which underscored the first three verses, beginning with the image of Jesus. This brings me to my interpretation of the song, and the title's meaning. The 'one' that Cave addresses in the first three verses is his inner God – anticipating her presence and the revelation she will provide that a Christian God cannot. As already explained, the fourth verse belittles the idea that she'll be able to provide such revelation. The final verse introduces a Christian God, and when Cave suddenly ends with the question 'Are you the one that I've been waiting for?', we have to ponder who is being addressed: the God within or a Christian God? The confusion regarding who 'the one' is, and the song's overall irresolution leave the listener in the dark.

'Where Do We Go Now But Nowhere?' (Cave) (5:46)

The return of acoustic guitar and the exotic passing chord that comes at the end of each phrase with the opening images of 'carnival drums' and 'grim reapers', suggests this is about Cave and Viviane Carneiro's crumbling marriage. A girl who was once 'So bold and so bright/Loose-limbed and laughing', is now a 'Ravaged avenger with a clip in your hair'; an extra layer of pain and sorrow provided by Warren's aching violin lines. The refrain is incredibly tender, as Cave pleads for his lover to 'wake up', suggesting the collapse of their marriage is akin to a nightmare. But other images give a different message – lines like 'If they'd give me my clothes back, then I could go home/From this fresh, this clean, antiseptic air' perhaps hearken back to his time in rehab, albeit the portrayal suggests it was like being in a mental institution.

Maybe their marriage felt like being locked away in a mental institution, walking around the duck pond 'One more doomed time and without much hope', with the prospect of going nowhere.

'West Country Girl' (Cave) (2:45)

The piano, which has featured on every song so far, is absent in place of an acoustic guitar, aided by violin, bass and percussion. This is very obviously about PJ Harvey, with references to her 'crooked face', 'heart-shaped face' and 'eyes of green'. His desire for her is conveyed not only through vivid recollection but through the folky musical accompaniment referring to her West Country home of Dorset.

'Black Hair' (Cave) (4:14)

What follows is another ode to PJ Harvey, or rather a fixated ode to her black hair, which Cave intimately romanticises about over the sparse accompaniment of subdued organ and Ellis' accordion. Her hair holds the weight of Cave's many descriptions, ranging from 'midnight black' to 'deep as ink' and 'black as the deepest sea'. While it may be 'charged with life' and physically invigorating – the smell of her hair staining his fingers – her hair is also deceptive and a keeper of secrets: 'All my tears cried against her milk-white throat/Hidden behind the curtain of her beautiful black hair'. It's incredible how much Cave can squeeze from one solitary image. But of course, the underlying sadness – or what Cave calls in *The Secret Life of the Love Song*, 'duende' – exposes itself near the song's end when she takes a 'train to the West'. Her departure seems final and irreversible.

'Idiot Prayer' (Cave) (4:21)

Perhaps the album's most out-of-place track, this is the only character-based one, as the protagonist speaks to the lover he murdered before he must face his imminent execution. He outlines his inner torment regarding his fate in either Heaven or Hell: one of which houses his murdered lover. Either way, he believes they will meet again. The final verse is the most compelling, as he sends his lover 'an idiot prayer of empty words': a peace offering 'sent on the wings of a dove', that's actually meaningless and cold. This is framed by perhaps the album's fullest band setup. Bargeld's guitar makes a more prominent appearance here, but this was the beginning of the end of his time in the band. Whilst I still enjoy the track and believe it doesn't devalue *The Boatman's Call*, it might've been better placed on an album such as *The Good Son*.

'Far From Me' (Cave) (5:33)

Cave performs and analyses this song in *The Secret Life of the Love Song*, revealing that the first verse was written at the beginning of his affair with PJ Harvey, when he was in the throes of an intense and exciting new love: 'For you, Dear, I was born/For you I was raised up'. However, Cave has said, 'The song – as if waiting for the inevitable traumatic experience – simply refused to let itself be completed until the catastrophe had occurred': the catastrophe being the eventual relationship breakdown. In this sense, the song's changing identity mirrors that of the lamented relationship – beginning with melodramatic assertions of romance, and slowly moving towards bitterness: 'You were my brave-hearted lover/At the first taste of trouble went running back to mother'. Each verse ends with the refrain 'Far from me', suggesting his lover has always been distant to an extent, whether that be mentally or, later on, physically. Ellis' violin-playing is once again an integral part, giving the refrain a sense of urgency. The wash of slide guitar that arrives is also very beautiful, especially when paired with the violin.

'Green Eyes' (Cave) (3:32)

Leonard Cohen comes to mind when I hear this beautiful closer. With piano providing the bedrock, we have sweet acoustic guitar panned closer to one side and melodica to the other, as Cave not only wearily sings, but his deep and stirring voice narrates on a separate track. One particular line always gets talked about – 'This useless old fucker and his twinkling cunt' – for obvious reasons. But Cave also spun a tale that it referred to musician Tori Amos sewing sequins into her pubic hair. This is obviously not true; rather the reference to PJ Harvey in the title gives away the real meaning, although the lover in the last verse could be anyone. The final lines before the refrain are poignant: 'Then leave me to my enemied dreams/And be quiet as you are leaving, Miss'. Cave desires for his lovers to leave quietly, whoever they may be or whoever may come next; to almost exit his life unnoticed so he doesn't have to battle with the feelings causing the album's torment. He simply wants to move on and dream of better times rather than dwell on the present catastrophe. Masterful lyrics and gorgeous songwriting.

No More Shall We Part (2001)

Personnel:
Nick Cave: vocals, piano
Mick Harvey: guitar, string arrangement, drums
Blixa Bargeld: guitar
Martin P. Casey: bass
Warren Ellis: violin, string arrangement
Conway Savage: organ
Jim Sclavunos: drums, percussion
Thomas Wydler: drums
The Bad Seeds: backing vocals
Guest musicians:
Kate and Anna McGarrigle: vocals
Gavyn Wright, Patrick Kiernan, Jackie Shave, Simon Fischer, Rebecca Hirsch: violin
Bruce White, Gustav Clarkson: viola
Frank Schaefer, Lionel Handy, Naomi Wright: cello
Paul Morgan, Leon Bosch: contra bass
Recorded at Abbey Road and Westside Studios, London, September-October 2000
Producers: Tony Cohen, The Bad Seeds
Label: Mute Records
Release date: 2 April 2001
Chart positions: UK: 15, USA: 180, Australia: 4
Running Time: 67:47

The Bad Seeds now entered a strange decade, characterised by a string of disjointed albums that don't live up to their last three 1990s albums. It was always going to be a mean feat following up the intense magnitude of *The Boatman's Call*. It's no wonder Cave put down his pen for a while after that, as explained in a 2001 *Daily Telegraph* interview: 'I'd gone through a bit of a slump after *The Boatman's Call*. I wasn't blocked, but I felt a bit disgusted with the whole thing and I didn't really feel like writing'. This begs the question: what was Cave doing in the four-year period between *The Boatman's Call* and *No More Shall We Part*, the band's longest break.

The biggest change in Cave's life came with his marriage to fashion model Susie Bick in 1999. He first met her at a fashion show at the V&A Museum in London, and Cave instantly fell in love, as detailed in the same *Daily Telegraph* interview: 'I thought she was the most beautiful woman I had ever seen in my life. And she continues to be. Even elbow-deep in baby shit, she looks pretty good to me'. The latter half of this statement exposes the other big change in Cave's life – in 2000, Susie gave birth to twins Earl and Arthur, making Cave the father of four boys: Luke, with Carneiro, and Jethro with Beau Lazenby, although Cave didn't meet Jethro until he was around seven years old.

With a wife and more children to look after, Cave's lifestyle also had to change. By the time he married Susie, he'd quit drugs and alcohol for the last time; the days of frantic drug-fuelled writing sessions were well and truly over. Instead, the chaos had been replaced with order and routine, as Cave began to approach his role as a musician much like a full-time office job – and I don't say this lightly, as he actually did acquire an office to work in, complete with an old Steinway piano which was a wedding gift from Susie's parents. The next album was written within the confines of this office, six days a week from nine to five.

The result was a natural extension of the sparse, downbeat piano-driven offerings on *The Boatman's Call*, albeit some of the tracks here have a little more charge. But if *The Boatman's Call* was born out of heartbreak, the lyrics here are more open to the world rather than being so focused on the self. Unsurprisingly, much of it seems to be informed by his marriage to Susie, love now being something more trusting and full of wonder, in contrast with the splintering pain it caused on *The Boatman's Call*. The band dynamic continued to evolve, with Warren Ellis's violin and string arrangements being very prominent. Harvey also helped with the string arrangements, though not as much as before *The Boatman's Call*; the same going for Bargeld, whose inimitable guitar sounds are absent and seemingly unnecessary for Cave's romantic laments. The vocals are also much stronger here, not to mention the higher vocal register adopted for the album.

Though *No More Shall We Part* was reviewed favourably, it's often been overlooked in the shadow of its mighty predecessor. There are many things to love about this album – the string arrangements are some of the band's best, Cave's voice is more assured, and the tracks have been carefully textured to create some of the most sorrowful of soundscapes. Interestingly, I find this to be less uplifting compared to *The Boatman's Call*, despite the lyrics being less wrought with personal despair and heartbreak. Instead, there's an underlying calm and melancholy that simmers gently and unobtrusively beneath Cave's hopeful and redemptive musings. For me, this is one of the Bad Seeds' stronger 2000s releases.

'As I Sat Sadly By Her Side' (Cave) (6:15)

We are plunged straight into the depths of the album's lethargic melancholy through the image of two lovers surveying the world outside their window as an innocent kitten dictates who will next share their thoughts regarding the state of the world. There is a beauty in the way the woman celebrates the common sadness of humanity: 'All are there forever falling/Falling lovely and amazing'. The man shares a more cynical view that portrays the falling of humanity to be clumsy and grim: 'Witness the man reaching up from the gutter/See the other one stumbling on who does not see'. This is backed by jangling guitar, soft brushes and a sorrowful piano. A beautiful string section adds a sense of urgency beneath the man's thoughts and the woman's reply in which she surmises that God doesn't care 'for those who sit at windows/In judgement of the world he created/While sorrows pile up around him/Ugly, useless and overinflated'. The woman basically rebukes the man for his miserable pessimism.

'And No More Shall We Part' (Cave) (4:00)

I can imagine this being played at some moody jazz cabaret evening, the weary piano chords underscored by bass and subtle brushes. The lyric seems to recount an unhappy marriage in which the narrator's wife appears entrapped by contracts and a ring 'locked upon the finger.'. There has obviously been conflict in the past ('All the hatchets have been buried now'), but there's a sense that the wife has been defeated in this war – her 'chain of command has been silenced now', therefore she has lost her own free will. The line 'Lord, stay by me' introduces the strings, and the mood is lightened by a more hopeful chord progression. It feels like we are hearing from the wife, who pleads for God to stay with her despite the harsh truth that she 'never was free' and 'will never be free/If I'm not free now': an attempt to make the best of a bad situation. The vocals of the McGarrigle sisters supports this theory, their voices adding a sweetness to this uplifting section before we finally end with that sinister line of inescapable ownership: 'And no more shall we part'.

'Hallelujah' (Cave, Ellis) (7:48)

We begin with a majestic ascending violin figure that acts as a grounding motif over bass and piano. This is a real tearjerker, as we encounter a man with some form of mental illness, conflicted through his inability to stay at home and his fear of the outside world. After giving his 'nurse the weekend off', he makes the most of being left to his own devices, and leaves his home unaccompanied, burdened by what his nurse would think of him leaving without his coat and accepting the invitation into a stranger's home. After concluding that his nurse 'had been my one salvation', he decides to return home. The difficulty of belonging anywhere causes him immeasurable pain: 'The tears are welling in my eyes again/I need twenty big buckets to catch them in'. The delicate voices of the McGarrigle sisters grace these lines, almost soothing the despair that radiates from them.

'Love Letter' (Cave) (4:08)

The tissues will be required again, as we're submerged in one of the album's most lush and romantic string arrangements, along with Cave's elegant piano melodies . It's a simple story – the narrator tells his lover something he regrets, and sends a letter to rectify things. But it's the sending of a physical carrier of one's thoughts and feelings that Cave is enamoured with. He explains the power of the love letter – and also the love song – in *The Secret Life of the Love Song*:

> Both serve as extended meditations on one's own beloved. Both serve to shorten the distance between the writer and the recipient. Both hold within them a permanence and power that the spoken word does not ... But more than that, both have the insidious power to imprison one's beloved, to bind their hands with love lines, gag them, blind them – for words become the

defining parameter that keeps the image of the loved one imprisoned in a bondage of poetry.

The physicality of the act – the way in which the narrator kisses the 'cold, white envelope' and presses his lips 'against her name' – alludes to what Cave says about the love letter shortening the distance between lovers. The line 'Rain your kisses down in storms' almost acts as a reply to the narrator's initial smooch. Cave's ability to find so much meaning in an object is a testament to his title of love balladeer.

'Fifteen Feet Of Pure White Snow' (Cave) (5:36)

This is perhaps the album's most well-known track and also the closest to a rock song. The quieter sections between Cave's vocals present an interplay between piano and pizzicato violin. The guitars are given room to breathe with warm scrapes and judders blessing each ear. The track then frantically builds at the refrain, eventually climaxing with the phrase 'O my Lord'. Lyrically this is not as straightforward as has been the case so far. Many fans suggest it's about excessive drug use, 'snow' being a slang term for cocaine – 'I've been paralysed by a lack of feeling'; 'Is there anyone else who feels this low?'. Cave's questioning of where everyone has gone, highlights the isolation of drug use. The Biblical names referenced could also suggest a loss of faith due to drug use.

However, the music video – which I must say is the best Bad Seeds music video ever – sees the band with famous faces like Jason Donovan, Jarvis Cocker and Noah Taylor partying in a room before suddenly transitioning into a synchronised line dance in the climactic sections. This suggests the song is about the Soviet Union, as the video opens with Russian writing beneath setting snapshots. Pictures of what look like important members of the communist party hang behind the band as they perform during the party. Lines like 'My neighbour waved to me/But neighbour is my enemy' perhaps refer to the Cold War and the widespread distrust during the time of communism. There's a lot to unpack, but, regardless, it's a true album highlight.

'God Is In The House' (Cave) (5:44)

Calm, serene, gentle; this track is a like a warm, fluffy pillow, with piano again being the dominant presence, aided by bass, soft drums, a fluttering tremolo guitar, and later on, Ellis' beautiful violin: all as minimally as possible. Here Cave provides a satirical criticism of Christianity and institutional religion, depicting a small insular town hiding itself from the sins of the world; the 'Homos roaming the streets in packs/Queer-bashers with tyre jacks', in their pure little church, which is 'painted white'. However, it becomes clear that these people are just as right-wing: 'That stuff is for the big cities' doesn't disapprove of such values, but rather these people attempt to use their church as a way of negating those same values that they share with the people in the big cities. The town is also very racist: 'We've bred all our kittens white/So you can see them in the night', but they falsely display a picture of equality by having a 'woman for a mayor'. I find the line 'Moral sneaks in the White House' incredibly clever as it epitomises the entire meaning – 'White House' also referring to their church painted white.

'Oh My Lord' (Cave) (7:30)

Another of the more energised tracks, this is a slow burner, beginning with piano and voice before everything else is gradually layered in and the overall intensity grows. By the end, the sonic palette becomes gloriously saturated with dramatic noise: overdriven guitar, clattering drums, aggressive piano and Ellis' intense ascending violin.

The lyrics deal with Cave's difficulty traversing life as a successful musician, and the media intrusion that follows him around: 'I thought I'd take a walk today/It's a mistake I sometimes make'. The media's powerful ability to distort identity is clear in the lines 'They claimed that I had lost the plot/Kept saying that I was not/The man I used to be', resulting in a feeling of going insane: 'Now I'm down on my hands and knees/And it's so fucking hot/Someone cries, 'What are you looking for?'/I scream, 'The plot, Baby, the plot!''. The frantic intensity reflects a feeling of reality crumbling around you as you start to lose not only a sense of yourself but your family as a result of such power.

'Sweetheart Come' (Cave, Adamson) (4:58)

In this beautiful love song, the narrator calls for his lover's burdens to be put aside, asking instead for her to 'Walk with me now under the stars/It's a safe and easy pleasure'. It's another of the more-muted tracks, reduced to piano and strings mainly, with the addition of background guitar and a solid rhythm section. The McGarrigle sisters feature on the chorus, and Ellis' violin again graces us with its presence, providing beautiful lines before each new verse.

'The Sorrowful Wife' (Cave) (5:18)

The arrangement is similar to the previous track; the emphasis on piano and strings until we're bombarded with an unexpected burst of raucous energy in which the overdriven guitars take charge and Cave's vocal becomes intense and aggressive. This is obviously about Susie, who he 'married on the day of the eclipse'. The line about her 'shifting the furniture around' is a direct reference to her eccentric habit of restlessly rearranging the furniture in the house. Despite being about Susie – and as the song title suggests – not everything is as happy as it should be, and the pivotal line 'I made her a promise I could not deliver' suggests this is the cause of her sorrow. Perhaps in the throes of initial love, he appeared to be the perfect man, but since their marriage, he's not delivered the promise of perfection she once saw. I love the contrast between the calming nature images in the reflective opening half ('Now we sit beneath the knotted yew/And the bluebells bob up around our shoes'), and nature's destructive, raging power ('A loose wind last night blew down/Black trees bent to the ground'), communicated in the crazed second half, where Cave becomes desperate for redemption: 'Help me now/I was blind/I was a fool'. You can really feel his world collapsing at this point.

'We Came Along This Road' (Cave) (6:08)

The instrumentation here is almost identical to the previous couple of tracks, and I can really hear this as an extension of *The Boatman's Call* with its focus on heartbreak. I believe that the lines 'wife's lover's smoking gun' and 'guns blazing at my hip' are used as analogies for the narrator's violent temper: bullets being replaced by hurtful words. As a result, he leaves 'by the back door' and hits the road, reflecting on how she was the one and nobody could compare. But then, 'We came along this road' – a road paved in violence and aggression.

'Gates To The Garden' (Cave) (4:09)

Overall, this is more hushed and sweeter than the previous track's melancholy. Cave reflects on our own mortality as he lists (as he's done a lot on this album) the many poor souls that lie beneath the ground of the churchyard he sits in: 'Fugitive fathers, sickly infants, decent mothers/Runaways and suicidal lovers…', the list goes on. But this morbidity is overpowered by the incredibly romantic image of the narrator's lover, 'Alive and leaning on the gates of the garden' – prompting the narrator to put aside the thoughts of the dead: 'For God is in this hand that I hold/As we open up the gates of the garden'. In contrast to the funeral for love in 'People Ain't No Good', love manifests itself in the garden: a place connoting life, beauty and growth. Like his God, Cave has a renewed faith in love, welcoming it rather than giving up on it.

'Darker With The Day' (Cave, Ellis) (6:07)

The closing track has a bit of everything, as the narrator paints a grim picture of the world on his 'final walk', which already sounds ominous. Some sort of loss is one cause of the narrator's turmoil. The chorus not only suggests that the narrator has lost a lover (It has been suggested that she's passed away), but in the context of the church that the narrator finds himself in ('seeking the presence of God' in the previous verse), this could otherwise suggest the narrator has lost a spiritual connection with his inner God. His personal problems sit alongside his despairing view of the people who walk the streets: 'Amateurs, dilettantes, hacks, cowboys, clones/The streets groan with little Caesars, Napoleons and cunts'. Overall, he's in a bad place, missing someone, hating everyone, and 'Full of a longing for something' that he can't pinpoint. It's perhaps the album's darkest track, masked by an accompaniment which is just as muted and lethargic as the previous tracks, though certainly not as melancholy – an interesting way to end.

Nocturama (2003)

Personnel:
Nick Cave: vocals, piano, Hammond organ
Mick Harvey: guitar, backing vocals, organ, acoustic guitar, bass, bongos, triangle
Blixa Bargeld: pedal steel, guitar, backing vocals, inexplicable guitar, gated guitar
Martyn P. Casey: bass
Warren Ellis: violin
Conway Savage: backing vocals
Jim Sclavunos: drums, backing vocals, percussion, tambourine
Thomas Wydler: drums, brush snare, shaker
Guest musicians:
Chris Bailey: chorus vocals ('Bring It On')
Johnny Turnbull, Mickey Gallagher: backing vocals ('He Wants You', 'Bring It On',
'There Is A Town', 'She Passed by My Window')
Norman Watt-Roy, Chas Jankel: backing vocals ('He Wants You', 'Bring It On' and
'There Is a Town')
Recorded at Sing Sing, Melbourne, March 2002
Producers: Nick Launay, The Bad Seeds
Label: Mute Records
Release date: 3 February 2003
Chart positions: UK: 20, USA: 182, Australia: 8
Running time: 57:35

We come to possibly the worst Bad Seeds album to date. Not to say it's entirely awful, but it's a far cry from the genius of past and future albums. It's an album that fans mutually regard as a blip in Cave's career – so much so that many asked Cave through his Q&A site *The Red Hand Files* to explain why *Nocturama* is so 'bad'. His response in issue 20 was humorous yet elegant:

> *Nocturama* is held in such universal contempt that its very title has become a byword for failure or disaster. 'He tried his best, but ultimately he met his *Nocturama*' you may hear someone say, or perhaps, 'What a complete and utter *Nocturama!*'. As the years have passed, the disdain for this record has not diminished, and nocturama has become just another word for 'loser' – as in 'Fuck you, you fucking *Nocturama!*'. And still, it continues to this day, so that when a Bad Seeds fan gets poked in the eye or kicked in the nuts, they cry, '*Nocturama!*'.

In the past, Cave has been known for getting satisfaction from controversy, and this is no exception, as he goes on to say he personally likes the record for the fact that it divides and upsets his fans. He also makes the essential point that this is the band's only severe blip, and that failure is imperative in order to learn and progress.

So what happened? Well, the record was composed under the same circumstances as the previous one: Cave nestled away in his office with a piano and a typewriter, working five or six days a week, often rising from his slumber at five am. By 2002, Cave, Susie and the twins had made their home in Sussex. He was a settled-down family man who no longer resembled the restless and placeless Cave of the 1980s and 1990s.

It feels like Cave created the album because it was his job, as opposed to constructing a set of songs that would progress the sound of the band further. Just the speed of the process communicates a message of nonchalance and almost carelessness in the way he approached the recording and releasing of the music here. The band learnt the songs and recorded the album in just seven days. Often each song only needed one or two live takes and that would be that – in contrast to how they previously worked, which involved copious amounts of time. Then again, Cave needed a break from the seriousness of his previous two albums, and didn't want to create something that would be as over-analysed. Harvey said the band purposefully set out to create a 'lightweight' record in that respect.

The sound had already drastically changed on the previous two records as Cave carried on scrubbing away the 'goth' stain that he loathed. The highly personalised style he'd adopted for those records bled through onto *Nocturama*, though he presents himself in a simpler manner. Furthermore, there's a return to the full-band setup that had been mainly absent from the last two records, and before its release, *Nocturama* was reported to sound like how they used to do it. With Cave and Harvey's reunion with producer Nick Launay – who 21 years previously had worked with The Birthday Party – it seemed likely that the band would return to their noisy thrash beginnings.

And so they did, and so they didn't: I'm not really sure what the focus was. While there are definitely flavours of the old Birthday Party sound, there's also a mishmash of styles recalling different Bad Seeds periods, including the recent minimalist piano-driven style. I wouldn't call it consistent at all – while it has its fair share of good moments, there are just as many hairy moments. Overall, there's nothing new on offer, as the band regurgitate their original familiar sound without doing it justice.

It's no wonder this was Blixa Bargeld's final Bad Seeds album before he left to focus solely on his other band Einstürzende Neubauten. This can't have been a surprise to anyone due to his diminishing role in the Bad Seeds in recent years. As a unit, they were changing, but the one thing they struggled for was a musical identity. The patchy *Nocturama* certainly confuses such an identity, and should be viewed as non-essential.

'Wonderful Life' (Cave) (6:49)

'It's a wonderful life' – perhaps one of the most clichéd lines in the history of clichéd lines, and to that end, I would never have expected to hear it from the lips of Nick Cave. But alas, he has the lot – wife, kids and a place to call home –

so why shouldn't he sing about the wonderful life he has? As you would expect with Cave, this isn't what it seems – in his forlorn voice, he communicates his dubiousness regarding the attainment of true happiness: 'It's a wonderful life/ If you can find it'. There's a deeper meaning in which he muses that the secrets acting as impenetrable barriers between lovers render the idea of a wonderful life unachievable. But I also like to think there's a humorous side to this, where Cave finds the domestic duties of family life horrifying. This is a good album starter and one of its stronger tracks – a natural extension of the previous album's languid sense of melancholy, with the piano being the dominant instrument – albeit it's a little more lively than most of *No More Shall We Part*. The Hammond organ injects menace whilst the guitar volume swells moan, adding a sense of sorrow.

'He Wants You' (Cave) (3:30)

The accompaniment behind Cave's aching love ballads has always been straightforward, and this is no exception. Gleeful, melodic piano, lush strings and a solid rhythm section make up this track, and while it's not his best love ballad, it is a beautiful composition. But the thing that's out of place are the lyrics, which to me feel uninspired and lacklustre. Cave's romantic images always conjure some deeper meaning brimming with multiple possible interpretations, and there's often a twist near the end. But here, there's no twist, and all we get are meaningless images of one lover rowing towards another: musically appealing but lyrically lacking.

'Right Out Of Your Hand' (Cave) (5:15)

This downbeat love ballad edges out the previous one. It's more muted, complete with slide guitar, Ellis' violin, and of course, the leading piano, which gives the chorus a jazz flavour: 'You've got me eating right out of your hand'. I believe the narrator – represented by the lion, which has connotations of strength and power – becomes hopelessly weak at the sight of his lover: 'the old lion yields'. Instead of being this ferocious animal that will bite your hand off, he instead submits and accepts her offer, whatever that may be. I love the line 'with your hand full of snow', as I can imagine the narrator's masculine feelings all melting away as a result of her warmth and tenderness.

'Bring It On' (Cave) (5:22)

The tempo is increased here. But I really don't like anything about this duet with singer Chris Bailey of The Saints (an Australian band that took the country by storm in the days of The Boys Next Door). For a man who has almost created his own music genre with his past material, this is a really poor songwriting effort. It sounds like a generic album-oriented rock song that you'd have on in the background during a car journey and forget about within seconds. The lyrics are not much better – a neglected garden is used as a metaphor for the lifeless state of a relationship, as the narrator asserts he'll take 'All your shattered dreams/And I'll scatter them into the sea'. If I were you, I'd skip this one.

'Dead Man In My Bed' (Cave) (4:40)
This is a better up-tempo track that can be compared to the thrashing charges of 'Janglin' Jack' and 'Deanna', but arguably is executed to a higher standard. Where those examples felt like throwaways placed on an album as an afterthought, this feels more assured, and it does justice to its garage rock style. Incessantly noisy guitars and the most ferocious Hammond organ are most noticeable. There's a little more space in the verses, but otherwise, everything is relentless from start to finish. The narrator examines a woman's troubles with her lover, who has become so numb and emotionally blocked that she describes him as a corpse. 'He used to be so good to me/Now he smells so fucking bad' and 'His eyes are open, but he cannot see' are my favourite lines. Overall, this is one of the album's stronger tracks, but it just seems out of place.

'Still In Love' (Cave) (4:44)
This album is certainly volatile, as we immediately return to a reflective and downbeat piano ballad narrated by a murdered husband. The killer's identity remains a mystery, but many speculate it was either the wife or the husband – both suggestions explaining the lines 'You might think I'm crazy/But I'm still in love with you'. The wife's emotional state changes with each verse. In the first, he observes her numbness at the crime scene ('Everybody's creeping around with plastic covers on their shoes/You're making coffee for everyone concerned'); in the second, he wishes she'd forget about him and move on ('Hide your memories, hide them all/Stuff them in a cardboard box'). In the third, we see her refreshed, full of life, and 'Without a solitary care', allowing the husband some closure as he falls asleep 'with no single memory of pain'. The track's sombre but not entirely miserable mood reflects this murder ballad's bittersweet ending.

'There Is A Town' (Cave) (4:58)
This is perhaps one of Cave's most accessible lyrics, as he yearns to go home to the place 'where I was born', which we all know is Australia – a place that feels mysterious: 'Far far away/Across the sea'. There's an amusing irony in that Cave once yearned for the opposite: to leave the place he was born and 'cross the sea'. This lyric is certainly not the most innovative, but sometimes simplicity is the key. Unfortunately, the music falls short for me, which is a shame, because there are some interesting things going on – especially the interplay between the weaving piano melody, the rhythmic guitar scuffles and Ellis' violin.

'Rock Of Gibraltar' (Cave) (3:00)
This is a widely-hated song, and I can see why. Typically, its unpopularity among fans fuelled Cave's decision to play it on every date of the album

tour. We are presented with three unremarkable minutes of dull, plodding accompaniment and some of Cave's worst lyrics to date. He uses the Rock of Gibraltar as a metaphor for the narrator's immovable love for his partner. Everything seems rosy and heartfelt until Cave does his usual trick and injects the potential for betrayal as the track ends. This is a far cry from his usual standard of love poetry, and way too shallow and simple for my liking.

'She Passed By My Window' (Cave) (3:20)

Unfortunately, this too falls short. The words are again rather superficial: 'You gotta sanctify my love', the lovestruck narrator pleads as the stranger who stops at his window rejects his company and passes on by. Again, the accompaniment is tame and radio-friendly, Ellis' ascending violin figure being the only thing worthy of note.

'Babe, I'm on Fire' (Cave) (14:45)

The best has been saved till last – a rollicking near-15-minute epic that preludes the assured garage rock of later albums *Dig, Lazarus, Dig!!!* and Cave's two albums as part of Grinderman. Despite the length, the band jammed for around five minutes before capturing their first full play-through on analogue tape, and this ended up being the final version. Launay – oblivious to the fact the track was to be nearly 15 minutes long – recalled having to frantically run another reel of tape on another machine before the first one ran out, as the band had exceeded the 16 minutes available on the tape reel. He believes he missed about 15 seconds of the take, and justifiably – but lightheartedly – blames Cave for not informing him of the track's length.

Casey's seething, snarling bass line is glorious, constantly driving the track forward while chaos runs amok. That same vile, fuzzy Hammond organ sound from 'Dead Man In My Bed' returns, equally as menacing and unpredictable. Charged guitars and violin also fight for the spotlight on this huge, uncompromising production. Indeed, this would be worthy of an adult pantomime, as implied by the farcical music video, which pictures the band dressing up as the countless characters featured in the lyrics – by far the most Cave has ever included in a song. From 'Bill Gates' to 'the backyard abortionist', 'The man in the basement/That's getting a taste for it' to 'the lost astronaut', everyone is saying 'Babe, I'm on fire'. I imagine it's meant to be apocalyptic, but the main thing is that Cave exposes a fun, careless side of himself that's always been overshadowed by the miserable, gothic persona falsely imposed on him. I've never been so entertained by a Nick Cave track.

Abattoir Blues/The Lyre of Orpheus (2004)

Personnel:
Nick Cave: vocals, piano
Mick Harvey: guitar
Martyn P. Casey: bass
Warren Ellis: violin, mandolin, bouzouki, flute
James Johnston: organ
Conway Savage: piano
Jim Sclavunos: drums (*Abattoir Blues*), percussion
Thomas Wydler: drums (*The Lyre of Orpheus*), percussion
Guest musicians:
Åse Bergstrøm, Donovan Lawrence, Geo Onayomake, Lena Palmer, Stephanie
Meade, Wendy Rose: backing vocals
Recorded at Studio Ferber, March-April 2004
Producers: Nick Launay, The Bad Seeds
Label: Mute Records
Release date: 20 September 2004
Chart positions: UK: 11, USA: 126, Australia: 5
Running time: 82:30

Cave and the band – minus Blixa Bargeld – regrouped just over a year later
to start recording what would be their true return to form. If *Nocturama* was
Cave's lightweight record, the follow-up would be the complete opposite:
Cave's grandest and longest offering to date. Furthermore, if *Nocturama* was
an inconsistent hotchpotch of styles and flavours, this record aimed to separate
the raucous from the gentle, over two separate albums. *Abattoir Blues* houses
the louder children, powered by Sclavunos' drums. *The Lyre of Orpheus* takes
care of the quieter ones, Wydler taking charge of the drum kit. This double
album is everything *Nocturama* failed to be: fresh, focused and exemplary of
the Bad Seeds' abilities.

   At the time, many fans probably doubted that the band would be able to
bounce back from Bargeld's departure – he was after all an integral part of the
band for many years, injecting an avant-garde flavour with his unique guitar
employment. But as we've already established, Cave fans are privileged in that
the band rarely have missteps, and certainly weren't going to be phased by
Bargeld's departure.

   In fact, the opposite was true – there was a new energy within the band,
which now included a new member of the band James Johnston. With
Johnston on organ, and Harvey taking up Bargeld's guitar duties, the whole
chemistry of the band had changed and as a consequence, this rejuvenated
spirit was captured in the recordings. This was in part due to the way the songs
were composed. Usually, Cave favoured being a solitary writer, but in this
instance, he and select Bad Seeds members (aptly nicknamed the 'micro-seeds':
consisting of Jim Sclavunos, Martyn P. Casey and Warren Ellis) decamped to

Paris to flesh out Cave's ideas. Sclavunos was particularly enthused with this new way of working as detailed in a 2004 *Dazed & Confused* interview: 'In Paris, we were trying to put songs together out of thin air, and a lot of stuff came out of those few days'. The success of this writing retreat is reflected in the sheer amount of tracks that came to fruition – so many that the band needed two albums to house it all. Evidently, it was an enjoyable, creative time.

Launay recommended that the band record the new tracks in Paris' Studio Ferber, which boasted a huge wooden live room, and once Cave heard that the likes of Nina Simone and Serge Gainsbourg had recorded there, he was sold on the idea. It was a wise decision, as the band had never sounded so full and purposeful. The record's enormous energy is a testament to the studio and the live recording method opting for feeling over precision. What makes this more impressive is that – similar to *Nocturama* – this double album was recorded quickly, in just under two weeks in fact, which is difficult to believe, considering how superb the overall sound is.

The other integral part of this record that separates it from earlier Bad Seeds records is the inclusion of the London Community Gospel Choir. I can imagine the choir members – coming as they do from a religious background – being a little taken aback by Cave's lyrics, which are not always squeaky clean. According to Launay, at certain points on the record, you can hear the singers laughing in the background in response to some of Cave's lines while recording. Having the powerhouse of the Gospel Choir only added to the album's enormity. This isn't just boisterous rock 'n' roll – it's fun, hollering gospel rock.

On its release, the double album received widespread critical acclaim, many citing it as the band's rebirth. It certainly feels like the band reinvented themselves here. They were finally able to definitively move away from the style of the last two albums, creating a consistently energised album of raucous material whilst simultaneously restating their knack for constructing thoughtful and reflective songs. This double album may not be the best entry point for a beginner, but once you're familiar with the classic Bad Seeds sound, the album is essential.

Abattoir Blues
'Get Ready For Love' (Cave, Ellis, Casey, Sclavunos) (5:05)
We step into Cave's chapel of gospel delights, greeted by the full-throated soul of the gospel choir chanting 'Praise him!' while the band go full-throttle. Your ears will not be prepared for such a fuzzy and gloriously-intrusive racket. Everything feels exciting and re-energised, Cave's vocals delivered with a renewed potency. I wonder what the choir members thought when they heard Cave uttering blasphemous lines like 'Praise him till you've forgotten what you're praising him for': another one of his sly digs at institutional religion. In fact, most of the lyrics here are rather scathing of such a rigid faith that ultimately fails to reward with the revelation it promises. I love the line, 'Then

I was just hanging around doing nothing/And looked up to see his face burned in the retina of your eyes' – as if religious fanaticism has clouded the Christian's vision, restricting them in what they're allowed to believe.

'Cannibal's Hymn' (Cave) (4:54)

Initially, this sounds like it could've easily fit on the more gentle *The Lyre of Orpheus* – beginning quietly and mysteriously with bongos, piano stabs, a hypnotic bass line and a strange robotic guitar noise with a filter effect on it. Then the drums and Hammond organ enter, and suddenly there's a spikiness and an assertive punch. But this bluesy track stills feels quite restrained, straddling the border between this album's riotousness and the second's understated nature. No matter which compartment you put it in, it is an excellent track in which the narrator worries about the people his lover mingles with: 'Those heathens you hang with down by the sea/All they want to do is defrock you'. He suggests that if she's 'gonna dine with them cannibals', she'll get eaten: an analogy for rape. However, it becomes clear that the narrator – who plans to 'Sing songs with a happy ending' to her – is a hypocrite, as he too is one of those cannibals. Lines such as 'Let me unlock you' and 'Here is some moonlight to cloak us' suggest he's going to do the same. That strange, slimy guitar sound is very apt in this instance.

'Hiding All Away' (Cave) (6:31)

Another spiky track that epitomises the catchphrase 'The calm before the storm'. But this is a rather unsettled calm, characterised by a funk-inflected backing in which the guitars, organ and gospel singers disjointedly interject around the syncopated rhythm section. There are brief moments of unified charge, but they quickly transition back into uneasy tension until we finally reach the climax or the storm on the repeated line 'There is a war coming'. All Hell is unleashed as Cave and the gospel choir scream their lungs out in this breathtaking finale: I don't think I've ever heard something so intense from the band. The lyrics up until this point are rather cryptic – sometimes lewd ('You asked at the local constabulary', 'They leered at you with their baby blues/And rubbed jelly on their sticks') and sometimes amusingly pompous ('You walked into the hall of fame/And approached my imitators'). But as we follow the lover going from place to place trying to find the elusive narrator who has hidden away from the world, it becomes clear that she finds danger and corruption everywhere. Then, the final line about war is either a warning or a battle cry against such corruption. This is definitely the centrepiece of this first album.

'Messiah Ward' (Cave) (5:14)

Being the most downcast and sombre track so far, this could easily fit on *The Lyre of Orpheus*. The gentle bass-and-guitar gallop keeps it from being languid, but it's certainly a far cry from the riotous opener. The descending piano melody bookending the track is stunning, and the gospel singers, instead of adding an enormity, inject an extra sense of sorrow into Cave's imagining of a post-apocalyptic world in which 'The stars have been torn down' and 'They're bringing out the dead, now'. The narrator's attempts to make sense of the situation – 'We could navigate our position by the stars' and 'We could comprehend our condition by the moon' – are hopeless, as the nature he once knew has been eradicated. All they can do is 'Look away' from the death and destruction.

'There She Goes, My Beautiful World' (Cave) (5:17)

This one is a little more upbeat, and sounds rather cheery and celebratory in the chorus. Cave muses on the subject of writer's block – a more-lighthearted focus in contrast with something as heavy as the thought of apocalypse. A cast of famous writers make an appearance: John Wilmot, Philip Larkin and Karl Marx, to name a few. Cave even includes the Ramones' Johnny Thunders, who 'was half alive when he wrote 'Chinese Rocks''. According to Cave in a 2004 *Dazed & Confused* interview, 'The song is just asking, 'How did these people do it? How did Johnny Thunders write 'Chinese Rocks'?', which is one of the greatest drug songs. Obviously, there was a certain humour to including him in that list, but I think I've got a certain talent for pulling those lines out on occasion'. Cave writes about the conditions under which these writers crafted some of their most powerful work – whether whilst battling a disease, in prison, or simply slaving away in a library – and he desperately wishes for the muse that *they* had in order to become unstuck from the creatively barren rut he finds himself in. There are two ways to interpret the chorus line 'There she goes, my beautiful world' – it could either reference the feeling of wanting to give up as his feminised muse disappears or instead of 'there she goes' representing a movement away, it could symbolise an excited, sudden burst of creative progress – it depends on the tone of the line but the uplifting, major chorus makes me believe the latter.

'Nature Boy' (Cave, Ellis, Casey, Sclavunos) (4:54)

The incredibly infectious chorus here places a lover in conjunction with the beauty and life of nature. The song certainly seems autobiographical – Cave recalling a 'routine atrocity' that he witnessed on TV in his youth, to which his father balanced the horror of such a crime with the beauty of the world, advising Cave that 'In the end, it is beauty that is going to save the world, now'. Cave finds this beauty within his wife Susie, and upon meeting her, has 'thoughts that were not in my best interest to mention': one of Cave's cheekier lines. Nature is also hailed for its beauty, and perhaps the 'she' in the chorus refers to nature: the sparrows, the sea, the flowers, the breeze, nature moves among all of these, and for Cave, moves 'something deep inside of me'. The music is just as uplifting as the subject matter – another lively, happy sing-along.

'Abattoir Blues' (Cave, Ellis) (3:58)

Backed by a punctuated drum rhythm and sustained piano chords, Cave again ruminates on apocalypse, albeit with a healthy dose of humour. Yes, 'abattoir' strikes up images of a slaughterhouse, and Cave seems to suggest we are all embarking on that journey towards the abattoir. But while his apocalyptic images grow ever more intense ('The sky is on fire/The dead are heaped across the land'), I can't help but smile when I hear the line, 'I woke up this morning with a frappuccino in my hand' – suggesting the threat of apocalypse is not superficial, but rather is hidden beneath a commercial reality that gives the false impression of everything being fine and rosy. 'Is there some way out of here?', he asks as he desires to be the Superman that saves the world from the apocalypse he outlines.

'Let The Bells Ring' (Cave, Ellis) (4:26)

This is dedicated to the late, great Johnny Cash: a figure of great significance for Cave. Cash shaped Cave's musical taste in his youth, showing him a darker side to rock 'n' roll that Cave obviously adopted for his own image and music. Cave covered Cash's 'The Singer' on *Kicking Against the Pricks*, and Cash even covered Cave's 'The Mercy Seat'. The way Cave describes an encounter with the man, reveals a great deal about this track: 'In early 2000, I saw Johnny Cash walk into a studio in L.A. – old and ill and temporarily blind – sit down and sing a song, then transform into a higher being.'

Cave witnessing Cash's transformation into a 'higher being' corresponds with the God-like depiction of Cash on this track: 'He is the real thing' Cave asserts in the chorus. Cash's grandiosity can't be matched by anyone – 'There are those of us not fit to tie the laces of your shoes' – and in comparison to his magnificence, we are all 'awed and mediocre'. It's a fitting tribute to a musical legend, with an accompaniment that's mainly acoustic in the verses, Ellis' florid mandolin standing out. The chorus is just as grand as the man it hails, with Hammond organ adding a fullness and an intensity to this joyful chant.

'Fable Of The Brown Ape' (Cave) (2:45)

I find this almost hearkens back to the blues-driven *The Firstborn Is Dead*, though the composition quality here is miles better. For this album's final track, we are presented with a tale about Farmer Emmerich finding a brown ape in a barn. He also found a serpent and decided to bring them into the house and feed them. When the villagers found out, they took the serpent and chopped it open, 'And the ground soaked/In the milk of human kindness'. The ape apparently escaped, 'Clanking its heavy chain' around the ranges and lamenting its murdered comrade. I have absolutely no idea what this is supposed to mean if it means anything at all, but it is very odd. The gospel choir's thunderous entrance on the phrase 'So long', is breathtaking in its sudden and unexpected power, briefly striking at the end of each verse. Such stark dynamics make this an exciting end to an enthralling first half.

The Lyre of Orpheus
'The Lyre Of Orpheus' (5:36) (Cave, Ellis, Casey, Sclavunos) (5:36)

What better way to begin the gentler side of this double album than with a grotesque retelling of a Greek myth. Instead of Orpheus' lyre offering music beautiful enough to provoke nature's dance, here the music he plays from his self-made lyre – constructed from 'a lump of wood, a piece of wire/And a little pot of glue' – inspires death wherever it's played. Eurydice falls victim to its murderous sound, as her 'eyes popped from their sockets/And her tongue burst through her throat', and nature's creatures can't escape from it either: 'Birdies detonated in the sky/Bunnies dashed their brains out on the trees'. An unimpressed God knocks Orpheus down to Hell as a result, where he reunites with Eurydice, who threatens to stick his lyre up his 'orifice' if he dares to play it again. Perhaps Cave is trying to tell us something about the quality of modern music, but maybe not. The music is just as mischievous as Cave's demythologised story – featuring relentless angular guitar-playing, which is chromatic in the verses. By the end, these ornate repetitions transition into a strumming tornado, as Cave and the gospel choir repeat 'O Mama' until the fade.

'Breathless' (Cave) (3:13)

This was the final song to be written and is perhaps his most unconventional. For anyone still convinced that Cave is the king of everything gothic, you will be proven wrong here. Cave explains his thinking behind the track in this 2004 *Dazed & Confused* interview:

> It was an attempt, from my point, to write a song that didn't have a twist at the end. It was a celebration of nature and divinity, and it had a buoyant melody. I mean, it still sounds sad to me, but I think that's just something that lives in my voice no matter what I do with it. To me, songs like that that are obviously written as celebrations of things, always suggest the other side of it anyway.

If you hadn't already guessed from 'Little white clouds like gambolling lambs' and 'happy hooded bluebells', natural imagery dominates, and instead of something awful happening at the end, Cave is rejuvenated by the power of nature throughout. Acoustic guitar keeps it light and gentle but lively. Ellis' idyllic flute-playing is a welcome addition. According to Cave, Ellis recorded multiple flute tracks, and Launay manipulated them all, reversing the audio, detuning, and adding different modulation effects. The end result produced 'an incredibly fucked-up 14th or 16th-century-style ensemble', as Cave puts it. The manipulated, interweaving parts create a flurry of serene goodness, mirroring Cave's celebration of nature.

'Babe, You Turn Me On' (Cave) (4:21)

There's something incredibly sensual about this in contrast to Cave's previous love songs, which were usually saturated in loss and heartbreak.

Here, the action between Cave and his lover takes place within the confines of mother nature:

> I move stealthily from tree to tree
> I shadow you for hours
> I make like I'm a little deer
> Grazing on the flowers

The sexual undertone is made all the more explicit in the lines 'I put one hand on your round ripe heart/And the other down your panties'. This track brims with heat and desire, reflected in the accompaniment's country waltz. Despite its simplicity, the lines 'Babe, you turn me on/Like an idea/Like an atom bomb' (in which he imitates the noise of an exploding atom bomb at the end), are my favourites because of the powerful symbol of pent-up, explosive desire.

'Easy Money' (Cave) (6:43)

This seems to tell the story of a man 'sleeping rough', who has to sell his body to the rich narrator in order to make some easy cash:

> He kissed me on the mouth
> His hands they headed south
> With my face pressed in the clover
> I wondered when this would be over

The rich man is not a likeable character, as he mulls over the difficulties of being rich ('Money, man, it is a bitch/The poor, they spoil it for the rich'), whilst the poor man has to make money through indecent means. The chorus says it all – the narrator has copious amounts of money, and he can comfortably 'Rain it down' on the family and the house. But after all, he must be unhappy if he's cheating on his wife, and there is a desperation in the vocal and the sorrowful gospel choir that highlight this point. The Bad Seeds provide a sombre accompaniment driven by acoustic guitar, with the most captivating musical device being the ghostly verse strings which dip in and out abruptly as if being switched on and off.

'Supernaturally' (Cave) (4:37)

This track wouldn't go amiss on *Abattoir Blues*. and is undoubtedly this album's most charged, with its stabbing piano chords, guitar flurries and growling violin. The lyrics – like many on this album – are more difficult to decipher than the ones on the previous two records, which had a more direct style. Here they're shrouded in enigma, as Cave finds himself haunted by his lover who appears everywhere in his thoughts; she is there but not really there at all. In the chorus, he yells, 'Hey! Ho!/Oh baby, don't you go all supernatural on me/Supernaturally', as he yearns for a physical presence over the supernatural grip she has on him.

'Spell' (Cave, Ellis, Casey, Sclavunos) (4:25)

The theme here is similar to the previous track, as the narrator calls for his lover but does not know where she is. He says, 'I'm full of love/And I'm full of wonder/And I'm falling under your spell', as he's supernaturally affected by his distant lover. The spectral swirl of strings after each chorus adds to this sense of supernatural witchiness and there's something mischievous in the gentle skittish nature of the verse accompaniment: especially in the bass and pizzicato violin parts. Some of Cave's most intense natural imagery can be found here:

> Through the woods and frosted moors
> Past the snow-caked hedgerows
> I bed down upon the drifting snow
> Sleep beneath the melting sky

It's poetic, and I love how nature acts as a catalyst for the narrator's descent into his lover's spell.

'Carry Me' (Cave) (3:37)

Here we're catapulted into a whirlwind of jittering strings and wobbling piano, which dance around a solid rhythm section. This characterises the verses, where the gospel choir take part in a call-and-response with Cave. In the chorus, the whirlwind subsides, and a sense of hope is made clear through a major tonality on the phrase 'Carry me'. The lyrics are again ambiguous, but there's something transcendent and mystical in the lines 'Carry me away' and 'I heard the many voices/Speaking to me from the depths below'. There are also hints of God in lines like 'Come and drink of me/Or turn away' – a line that could be directed at Jesus' disciples – and when I hear 'The mystery of the word', that immediately makes me think of God. However, I can't focus these ideas – whatever it is, there's something spiritual at play.

'O Children' (Cave) (6:51)

The finale is the highlight of this album and probably the double album as a whole. A similar soundscape to the previous track is created, albeit the strings are more subtle and reserved in the background, and there is no uplifting chorus, a sense of grief sustained throughout. The lyrics are again cryptic, and I've heard a few different interpretations. The reference to the 'gulag' could suggest that this is about children in Nazi concentration camps. But I prefer an interpretation I read that said 'the cleaners' is a metaphor for time: 'You don't even want to let them start'. As the song progresses, characters such as 'Frank and poor old Jim' become older – 'The cleaners have done their job on you' – until 'Poor old Jim's white as a ghost', predicting his imminent death. But in death, their youthful spirits that were previously 'held in chains' and stuck in a material body ravaged by time, jump on the 'little train' departing for the kingdom of Heaven.

This song feels like a childhood lament; the angelic gospel voices calling out and empowering the youthful spirit: 'O children, lift up your voice'. It's close to perfection, and a song that's close to my heart.

Dig, Lazarus, Dig!!! (2008)

Personnel:
Nick Cave: vocals, organ, piano, tambourine, sleigh bells, toms, harmonica, electric guitar, vibra-slap
Mick Harvey: electric guitar, acoustic guitar, bass, organ
Martyn P. Casey: bass
Warren Ellis: viola, loops, Fender mandocaster, tenor guitar, maraca, 12-string lute, drum machine, piano, flute, mandolin
James Johnston: organ, electric guitar
Jim Sclavunos: drums, bongos, cowbell, cuica, congas, finger cymbal, shaker, maraca, tambourine, sleigh bells
Thomas Wydler: brushed snare, shaker, tambourine, drums, hand drums
Conway Savage: listed, but doesn't play his usual keyboards
The Bad Seeds: all backing vocals and handclaps
Recorded at State of The Ark Studios, London, June-July 2007
Producers: Nick Launay, The Bad Seeds
Label: Mute Records
Release date: 3 March 2008
Chart positions: UK: 4, USA: 64, Australia: 2
Running Time: 53:35

A lot happened in the four years between *Abattoir Blues/The Lyre of Orpheus* and *Dig, Lazarus, Dig!!!*. In 2005, Cave's scriptwriting came to prominence with the release of *The Proposition*: an Australian western directed by his long-term friend and collaborator John Hillcoat. Cave composed the soundtrack with Warren Ellis: their partnership becoming all the more solidified. Cave also reached the age of 50 in 2007, and that year he was inducted into the ARIA Hall of Fame, though he only allowed himself to be inducted on his own terms: 'I can't really accept this until we get a few things straight', he exclaimed, as he took it upon himself to also induct The Bad Seeds and The Birthday Party before accepting the honour.

But perhaps the most significant development was the 2006 formation of a filthy rock 'n' roll side project called Grinderman, made up of members from the micro-Seeds offshoot: Cave, Casey, Sclavunos and Ellis. The energy and power of *Abattoir/Lyre* is still present, but unlike its soulful gospel rock that housed complex and ambiguous lyrics, the sound of Grinderman's eponyous 2007 debut radiates rough and raw garage rock that hearkens back to the unholy noise of The Birthday Party – Cave even picked up a guitar for the first time. With a four-piece, he was able to do away with the cluttered and saturated sound of *Abattoir/Lyre*, instead using a smaller unit to create the same brutal power. The explicit lyrical content focuses on sex and is free from the weighty themes that characterised *Abattoir/Lyre*.

It was inevitable that the Grinderman influence would rub off on the Bad Seeds' next record, even if Cave didn't initially want that to happen. In hindsight, it was a move that paid off, as *Dig* was equally as applauded as *Grinderman*, and even appealed to a younger demographic. Sticking to their guns, the band went with the 'extremely raucous acoustic' sound they'd first conceived on *Henry's Dream*, in contrast to the electric, distorted nature of the Grinderman debut. The result of a mere five days of recording was Cave's most accessible, amusing and indeed funky record to date; the lyrics described as 'a haemorrhaging of words and ideas'. One only has to look through the lyrics to understand the uncontrolled and frantic writing style. Everything is disparate and untethered, some words capitalised, others wandering off the page. It's exciting and adventurous.

The album was greeted with unanimous praise – 'A triumph from first to last' according to Graeme Thomson of *The Guardian*. Stephen M. Deusner of *Pitchfork* gloriously asserted, 'This is how rock musicians are supposed to age'. It is a good album, but I prefer *Abattoir/Lyre*. This one doesn't live up to the mastery of past (and future) Bad Seeds albums. But it's certainly unique and represents another step away from the band's past musical styles. Sadly, despite the album's success, this would be Mick Harvey's final Bad Seeds album – him being one of the founding members and arguably the keystone that held everything together for years. The studio exposed the tension between Harvey and the new creative Cave/Ellis partnership. Where Harvey would turn things down, Cave and Ellis would turn things back up. Once Cave's main collaborator, Harvey's role had been dissolving over the decade, and he eventually announced his departure at the end of the album tour.

Released in 2009, Cave's second novel *The Death of Bunny Munro* – completely different in style to the archaic southern-gothic language of the first – is reflective of this seedy period, as it follows the pursuits of the lustful, beauty-product salesman Bunny Munro with his son Bunny Junior in tow. It's inappropriately funny and tragic. This and the second Grinderman album bring to a close this wildly outrageous and explicit identity that the band carved for themselves after *Abattoir/Lyre*.

'Dig, Lazarus, Dig!!!' (Cave) (4:11)

Powered by a machine-like rhythm and the band's robotic chants repeating 'Dig yourself, LAZARUS!!!!!!/DIG YOURSELF', we are plunged into Cave's Americanised world, housing a lost and confused Lazarus (Larry) who has risen from the dead. This is what Cave says on his website:

> Ever since I can remember hearing the Lazarus story when I was a kid – you know, back in church – I was disturbed and worried by it; traumatised, actually. We are all, of course, in awe of the greatest of Christ's miracle – raising a man from the dead – but I couldn't help but wonder how Lazarus felt about it. As a child, it gave me the creeps, to be honest. I've taken Lazarus and stuck him in New York City, in order to give the song a hip contemporary feel. I was also thinking about Harry Houdini, who spent a lot of his life trying to debunk

the spiritualists who were cashing in on the bereaved. He believed there was nothing going on beyond the grave. He was the second greatest escapologist, Harry was; Lazarus of course being the greatest. I wanted to create a kind of vehicle, a medium, for Houdini to speak to us if he so desires – you know, from beyond the grave.

Yes, Larry finds both fame ('Fame finally found him/Mirrors became his torturers/ Cameras snapped him at every chance') and destitution ('in a soup queue/a dope fiend/(a slave)/Then prison/Then the madhouse/Then the grave) as he completes a journey through different American cities, indulging in the delights of drugs and women, before finding himself dead again. I find the line 'There is definitely something going on upstairs' really interesting – 'upstairs' could represent the outside world above the ground Larry is buried in, or it could represent Heaven, and God's meddling with Larry's destiny: spoiling his eternal rest.

'Today's Lesson' (Cave) (4:41)

There's something incredibly groovy about this track that asserts in the chorus, 'We're GONNA HAVE A REAL COOL TIME TONITE!!!'. It's the party anthem I never thought I'd hear from the band, complete with Warren's wailing wah-wah *mandocaster*, Casey's rumbling bass and the inviting organ. Cave tells the story of Janie, who wakes up from a dream with a 'gun like a jawbone down the waist of her jeans'. Another character – Mr. Sandman – violates Janie in her sleep, and is later described as 'the inseminator' who 'opens her up like a love letter & enters her dreams'. This line is spaced weirdly in the complete lyrics book so that 'enters her' is somewhat separate from 'dreams'. It appears sexual but is desexualised by completing the sentence with 'dreams': an example of Cave's chaotic choice of form. I'm not sure if there's meaning behind this, and the lyrics are very difficult to organise and arrange, but there is a strange and twisted desire in the chorus that is rather discomforting.

'Moonland' (Cave, Ellis, Casey, Sclavunos) (3:53)

An insistent groove powers the percussion here, which includes a hand drum Ellis invented that creates a resonant wobbling sound. This is perhaps the closest the band have ever come to reggae. This track is not as intense and intrusive when compared with the majority of tracks on the album, but rather there's a slick charm behind the post-apocalyptic world the character enters. Reading some of the lyrics, Kurt Vonnegut's *Slaughterhouse Five* comes to mind – the narrator arising from a 'meat locker', mirrors the meat locker that Billy Pilgrim takes shelter in during the Dresden firebombing in Vonnegut's novel. Pilgrim departs from the meat locker in the aftermath of destruction, comparing Dresden to the moon, much like Cave's narrator describes wherever he is as 'Moonland' ... 'under the ash'. But there are contrary lines like 'I'm not yr favourite lover' and 'It must feel nice to know, that somebody needs you'. There are obvious relationship issues here, and the barren landscape reflects the narrator's loneliness and isolation.

'Night Of The Lotus Eaters' (Cave, Ellis) (4:53)

An interesting title, with an interesting accompaniment built around Ellis' percussive loop which acts as the backbone for the entire track. Around this loop, we hear the group improvising – moaning feedback, congas and random drum kit interjections create an eerie atmosphere. It's possible that the lotus-eaters represent the 'catastrophic leaders' and life's other corrupt money-focused aspects that bring out the worst in people. Here, Cave calls for resistance: 'get ready to shield yourself!!!!!!!!!!/grab yr sap & yr heaters', fighting back against the frivolities of politics and commercialisation in order to retain some dignity and self-respect.

'Albert Goes West' (Cave, Ellis) (3:32)

Containing a barrage of fuzzy thrashing guitar, this is perhaps the album's most garage-rock-inflected track; moments of respite arriving in the form of more-sparse percussion. As the title suggests, there is some movement across America, through the guises of a few different characters, and all have a different story. The album's sexual undercurrent rears its head in lines like 'henry he went south & lost his way/deep in the weeping forests of le vulva'. Overall, each character's story is left unfinished and ambiguous.

'We Call Upon The Author' (Cave, Ellis) (5:11)

A fan favourite from the album, Ellis' loops are used to great effect here. The track is largely a straight-up rock song apart from two breaks during the song in which one of Ellis' funky, techno loops intercede out of nowhere. It sounds so alien – in part due to a metallic sound moving from left to right – that it's almost ridiculous against the main bulk of the track. But somehow, it works!

This is the hardest to try and lyrically organise. If you've already seen the lyrics in the complete lyrics book, you'll know it looks like someone has thrown up on the page. I believe that by 'the author', Cave means God, as the narrator calls on God to explain why there is suffering: 'o rampant discrimination/ mass poverty/ third world debt/ infectious/disease/ global inequality and deepening socio-economic divisions'. Cave boasts a few words that will have listeners reaching for their dictionaries, including 'myxomatoid', 'jejune' and 'prolix' – the latter being repeated in the line 'PROLIX!!!!/PROLIX!!!!/SOMETHING A PAIR OF SCISSORS CAN FIX!!!!!!!!'. The idea is that a pair of scissors can cut off the suffering that makes God's earthly novel overly long. Other amusing references and images randomly crop up, adding to the sheer chaos.

'Hold On To Yourself' (Cave, Ellis, Casey, Sclavunos) (5:50)

This country-like song is dominated by acoustic guitar and spaghetti-western-sounding electric guitar over effects sounding like violin harmonics. Distance between lovers is the talking point here, the narrator opening with '(I'm so far away from you)'. There's a sense that his lover is heading towards mental chaos and ruin ('well cities rust & fall to ruin/factories close & cars go cruising/in and around the borders of her vision') as he pleads for her to hold onto herself and not give into insanity while he's away. This all sounds very profound until you realise it's basically outlining the sexual frustration between these two characters.

'Lie Down Here (& Be My Girl)' (Cave) (4:57)

The theme of sexual frustration continues, evident in the lines 'it's a matter of urgency/o darling can't y/ see/ I can't hold back the tide'. There's a feverish obsession in the line 'I'd build a million of y/ baby/& every single one of them will be mine'. It's a song of longing and desperation, mirrored in the frantic and fierce accompaniment driven by acoustic guitar, made deranged by incredibly abrasive and fuzzy guitar wails.

'Jesus Of The Moon' (Cave) (3:22)

Regarding love ballads and the lack of them on this album, Cave said at the time, 'I was throwing out a lot of those marriage love songs around *Dig, Lazarus, Dig!!!*, and not pursuing them because I didn't want to write a record of that sort of stuff – I wanted to write a record with a lot of visceral energy'. This track is the exception, calling back to Cave's period as a crooning balladeer. There's obviously some sort of rift between the narrator and his lover, who is left behind 'curled up like a child' in the St. James hotel. The relationship demise is made inevitable, but there's no sense of melodramatic tragedy or regret – rather of new beginnings and moving away from the past: 'cause people often talk about being scared of change/but for me, I'm more afraid of things staying the same'. The music is sombre, but it certainly isn't stagnant: reflecting the narrator's desire to push forward with his life. There is also a tasteful flute solo from Ellis near the end.

'Midnight Man' (Cave) (5:06)

There are two characters that the narrator's lover desires: 'yr ever-loving man' and 'yr midnight man'. The narrator is the 'ever-loving man': the 'chrysalis' that is 'rearranging' itself constantly so that he resembles the perfect image of the man she has in mind. But he has to share the stage with the 'midnight man': her bit on the side that 'everybody wants to be'. It's rather sad, actually, as the narrator simply grits his teeth and allows this to happen. But by the end, we get a sense of his hopelessness: 'it's early in the morning/& it's happening again/I called y/ once/I called y/ twice/ain't I your midnight man'. Musically, the track is rather upbeat in contrast with the subject matter – a straight-up rock song with playful organ and one of Ellis' ambient loops underneath.

'More News From Nowhere' (Cave, Ellis, Casey, Sclavunos) (7:58)

In its hallucinatory style, the closer reminds me of The Velvet Underground: in part due to Ellis' dreamy loop beneath the sophisticated, lethargic accompaniment. A couple of lines are taken directly from Homer's 'Odyssey' – specifically 'he must be about 100 foot tall/& he only has one eye': referencing the land of Cyclopes – and the phrase 'wine-dark sea' is repeated multiple times in Homer's epic. There's probably a way the entire song can be manipulated to fit with the poem. But more generally, Cave is a wanderer, as he encounters familiar faces from the past – including 'Deanna' (who made an appearance on *Tender Prey*), 'Miss Polly' (a possible reference to PJ Harvey, whose presence was felt on *The Boatman's Call*), and a girl called Alina, who could represent Anita Lane. But it's the past that plays on Cave's mind here:

> dont it make you feel so sad
> dont the blood rush to yr feet
> to think that everything you do today
> tomorrow is obsolete

A rather pessimistic ending to an album that has otherwise been lewd yet entertaining.

Push the Sky Away (2013)

Personnel:
Nick Cave: vocals, piano, Rhodes
Warren Ellis: violin, viola, flute, tenor guitar, synthesizer, loops, Rhodes
Martyn P. Casey: bass
Conway Savage: vocals
Jim Sclavunos: percussion
Thomas Wydler: drums
The Bad Seeds: backing vocals
Guest musicians:
Barry Adamson: bass ('Finishing Jubilee Street', 'Push The Sky Away'), backing vocals
George Vjestica: 12-string guitar ('Jubilee Street', 'Mermaids'); backing vocals ('Mermaids', 'Higgs Boson Blues')
Chris Dauray: saxophone ('Higgs Boson Blues')
Jessica Neilson: bass clarinet ('Higgs Boson Blues')
Ryan Porter: trombone ('Higgs Boson Blues')
Antonio Beliveau, Aya Peard, Jason Evigan, Natalie Wilde: backing vocals ('We No Who U R', 'Water's Edge', 'Finishing Jubilee Street', 'Push The Sky Away')
Martha Skye Murphy: backing vocals ('We No Who U R', 'Water's edge', 'Finishing Jubilee Street')
Children of Ecole Saint Martin: backing vocals ('Jubilee Street', 'Higgs Boson Blues', 'Push The Sky Away')
Recorded at La Fabrique, Saint-Rémy-de-Provence, France, December 2011/August 2012
Producers: Nick Launay, The Bad Seeds
Label: Bad Seed Ltd.
Release date: 18 February 2013
Chart positions: UK: 3, USA: 29, Australia: 1
Running time: 42:40

Just as there was uncertainty among Cave fans following the departure of Bargeld after *Nocturama*, a similar sort of trepidation was felt after Harvey's departure following the release of *Dig, Lazarus, Dig!!!*. Furthermore, after the release of *Grinderman 2* in 2010, Cave had stated that his raucous offshoot band were to take a rest from recording (though in more recent years, he's teased the possibility of a third Grinderman album). With Grinderman's raw, visceral, energy on the back-burner and Warren Ellis officially becoming Cave's right-hand man, the band were in a position to challenge fans with something completely new – as Cave put it in a 2013 interview with *The Guardian*: a 'move away from guitar-orientated music and that classic Nick Cave ballad style, to let a little bit of air and a little bit of light in'.

But the new album's construction didn't differ much from the approach taken with the last Bad Seeds album and the two Grinderman albums: 'It's very much informed by the working methods of Grinderman – a kind of reduction of things, an attempt to make the music as lean as we possibly can. It's about space within the music'. Indeed, what put these albums in contrast to the equally charged *Abattoir/Lyre*, was an economical approach that rewarded the same punch without the need for saturation. Although *Push the Sky Away* may sound entirely alien to *Dig*, it should be regarded as an extension of the band's textural experimentation.

On *Push*, the band sort of came full circle: just as Cave went from the frenzied Old Testament preacher of the 1980s to the crooning piano balladeer of the late-1990s/early-2000s, a similar transition occurs between *Dig* and *Push*. But Cave's piano playing does *not* make such a bold return. For the next three albums, synthesizers – the possibilities of which were previously unchartered by the band – featured heavily during this ambient period.

Ellis' contributions were to be felt more than ever. Not only was he in charge of such synthesized sounds and the textures he could create with strings, but his ambient and airy loops also give this album an oceanic wave-like quality. Of course, there are a couple of tracks that are a little more energetic, but for the most part, everything is more repressed and muted than had been the case on the last two Bad Seeds records. Cave actually wrote a lot of the album material while surveying the ocean from his study in his Brighton home, which explains the album's meditative calm.

Cave's Brighton home also served as the backdrop for the striking cover art, which sees a naked Susie Bick being illuminated by the light that Cave welcomes in when opening a window shutter. Dominique Isserman took the photo while Susie was modelling for a shoot. Cave was helping, and Isserman told him to open the shutters. As this was happening, Susie dropped her robes and Isserman captured the moment.

The lyrics begin to move away from the narrative style Cave had adopted throughout his career, opting instead for a style closer to a stream-of-consciousness. *Push* has Cave ruminating on everything modern – the internet, texting, Wikipedia and even scientific discovery – navigating his way through a modern world: in other words, pushing the sky away.

The album was met with largely positive reviews. Many were quick to point out that fans of a more lively Cave might be disappointed with the minimalist, ambient approach taken on the album. Other reviews compared the album to *The Boatman's Call*, though to me, they are wildly different. This album begins perhaps my favourite Bad Seeds period – being the first of three albums where the band continue developing their use of ambient textures.

'We No Who U R' (Cave, Ellis) (4:04)

For how delicate and contemplative the track sounds, the subject matter is rather weighty, as Cave's ponderings on the state of the modern world begin with environmental concerns. He explains this in a 2013 *Filter* interview:

All songs have the capacity to collect weight around them, by the music and by the way that they're sung. To me, it is a huge song. It was not actually supposed to be an environmental song, but I'm quite happy for it to just be what it wants to be. It is a concern of mine. We've treated nature abominably, and it's getting back at us with a vengeance.

The trees – foreshadowing their destruction at the hands of humanity – are personified, as nature's vengeance is highlighted in the refrain 'And we know who you are/And we know where you live'. But the song title has an entirely different meaning – its text-speak suggests that the refrain (sung with a hushed backing chorus) could be directed at someone online; the trees possibly representing powerful figures who 'don't care what the little bird sings', and by the final verse 'will burn like blackened hands'. But these are anonymous online threats, and the calm and collected accompaniment behind Cave's whisper certainly reflects the ease of making such superficial threats.

'Wide Lovely Eyes' (Cave, Ellis) (3:40)

Scurried, muted guitar drives this track, with a warm Rhodes electric piano gently swirling around. The chorus – characterised by glassy synthesized splashes and a chorus of backing vocals – washes over like a wave. In terms of the rhythm section, Casey's bass is there but very much understated, as guitar predominantly keeps the tempo. Brighton's beach must have made an impression on Cave, as we get metaphors with the word 'wave': 'Crystal waves and waves of love' and 'The waves of blue and the waves of love' conjuring romantic sea images. But 'wave' also comes to mean the character's final goodbye, as she wishes to depart from a world that's no longer brimming with fun and laughter but rather is desolate and uninviting: 'They've dismantled the funfair/And dismantled the rides'. As far as suicide stories go, this one is rather joyous. The ocean she steps into is welcoming, beautiful and full of love.

'Water's Edge' (Cave, Ellis, Wydler) (3:49)

A galloping bass line holds together the feel of this track which sees each band member interject – random flurries of drums, piano, and the utterances of another bass in a higher register all fight for attention against a mournful, repeating violin line and one of Ellis' ambient loops. In the refrain, a gorgeous wave of strings washes over, before the menacing bass rumble resumes. This is more unsettling than the last two tracks, which is no surprise considering the theme of sexual violence. The 'girls from the capital' who come to the beach are preyed on by the local boys, who 'grow hard, hard to be heard'. Eventually, they 'seize the girls from the capital/Who shriek at the edge of the water'. Perhaps the most upsetting lines are, 'Their legs wide to the world like bibles open/To be speared and taking their bodies apart like toys'. In the previous track, the beach and sea acted as an empowering escape from the world, whereas here it is a grim place of voyeurism and horrible crimes.

'Jubilee Street' (Cave, Ellis) (6:35)

Arguably the album's best track, this is perhaps its most energetic. It begins with just drums, bass, and the chord progression that repeats throughout. Every few cycles, the song grows in intensity through the addition of acoustic guitar and cinematic strings, which themselves become more and more luxurious and grand. By the end, the guitar is dirtied-up, a distant-sounding choir adds to the drama, and Ellis' violin begins to screech and wail just as the fade begins.

Brighton again makes its presence felt, Jubilee Street being a road in Brighton, though Cave has given it a seedy backdrop, visited by corrupt individuals who 'ought to practice what they preach'. The protagonist Bee is a Jubilee Street prostitute who serves the needs of the narrator frequently: 'The problem was/She had a little black book/And my name was written on every page'.

Burdened by the thought of losing his respectability, it is indirectly suggested that the narrator murders Bee ('I got love in my tummy/And a tiny little pain/ And a ten-ton catastrophe/On a sixty-pound chain'), and by the end, the narrator is 'beyond recriminations', and 'transforming', 'glowing', 'vibrating': he is thriving in life now that he's unburdened himself.

'Mermaids' (Cave, Ellis) (3:49)

Cave has always been one for myths, 'The Lyre of Orpheus' being one example, and this track, another, although here Cave celebrates the power of the imagination in lifting our spirits from the disheartening trials and tribulations of mortal reality: 'I think the song 'Mermaids' is about a sort of spiritual collapse. The mermaids are myths and products of our imaginations, and it's about going somewhere that is separate from the world and being saved by our imaginations. It's a respite from the world'.

Entering a world in which mermaids exist proves to be a saviour from 'the husband alertness course' in which the narrator's wife no longer desires him:

I was the match that would fire up her snatch
But there was a catch
I was no match
I was fired from her crotch

Images of mermaids sunbathing on the rocks, waving to the narrator and gracefully slipping back into the sea give comfort to both the narrator and the listener.

The music is just as serene as these calming images. It begins with a lush tremolo guitar, as it swims more or less alone in the verses. At the chorus, a fuller washes over, complete with acoustic guitar, a sturdy yet delicate drum rhythm, and some of Ellis' most beautiful sounds: one of which resembles a whale noise.

'We Real Cool' (Cave, Ellis) (4:18)

Casey's galloping bass returns, sounding even more sinister than before, this time largely unsupported. There is a piano tinkle here and there, a slither of strings or a patter of toms, but the track is rather menacing in its sparsity. However, as it progresses, the strings and piano become prominent, creating beauty through their synergy. I believe the lyrics hail the achievements of science, as Cave sort of directs his questions towards the listener, quizzing us on our knowledge of the great scientists who made such breathtaking discoveries: 'Who measured the distance from the planets/Right down to your big blue spinning world?'. In fact, the lyrics sort of make me want to search Google for these answers, and what better place than Wikipedia: 'Wikipedia is heaven/When you don't want to remember no more'. It's a modern convenience that Cave expresses an interest in as explained in this 2013 *Filter* interview:

> I've always done an enormous amount of research, so I'm quite familiar with building up worlds around the songs. And Wikipedia is a wonderful device because it's there at your fingertips. It's unreliable, but it's poetic in that it's a cluster of information, some of it esoteric, which is a lot like songwriting itself. And for someone who writes highly-visual songs, it's the perfect place to go for just the kind of detail that has that shock-and-awe effect when placed within a song.

It is certainly novel to hear Cave sing the word 'Wikipedia', and even more so when he calls it 'heaven'. All in all, it's nice to hear Cave's appreciation of such important scientists, asserting that they are the 'real cool' people of the modern world.

'Finishing Jubilee Street' (Cave, Ellis, Wydler) (4:28)

This spoken-word piece references a dream Cave had after completing the writing of 'Jubilee Street'. In the dream, he married a young girl called Mary Stanford, and upon waking, he 'flew into a frenzy high and low' searching for her. A chilled-out groove frames this dream recollection, characterised by clunky percussion and relentless fingerpicked electric guitar. Other instruments dip in and out randomly, creating a rather hazy and hallucinogenic soundscape. The only moment of unity is on the refrain line 'See that girl comin' on down', sung by a gentle chorus of backing vocalists.

'Higgs Boson Blues' (Cave, Ellis) (7:50)

In 2011, the discovery of the Higgs particle – also known as the God particle – was celebrated as a remarkable achievement in the field of contemporary physics, one that supposedly filled in a huge gap regarding the universe's structure. But it was a bittersweet discovery that left physicists at a loose end over what to put their energies into next. The question is, did such a remarkable discovery change the world and will it impact the future of humanity? 'Who cares what the future brings?', exclaims the narrator, who is in his car driving down to Geneva – the place where the particle was discovered – as he surveys an unchanged world that is still, in Cave's mind, heading towards apocalypse: 'Flamed trees lie in the streets'. On this journey, the narrator encounters a whole cast of characters, including the Devil, blues guitarist Robert Johnson, Hannah Montana, Miley Cyrus, a missionary 'with his smallpox and flu', a man 'preaching in a language that is completely new' and there is an alluding to the assassination of Martin Luther King. With the writing style being very much a stream of consciousness, it's wildly open to interpretation. In my opinion, there's a desire to discover, the ultimate discovery being the particle (or in other words, God) in Geneva. However, these discoveries – no matter how frivolous or ground-breaking – will never reward us with a true sense of revelation. There will always be questions, and the meaning of life will always elude us, which is why this is a blues song.

The track follows the same blueprint as 'Jubilee Street', in that we are treated to nearly eight minutes of growth from humble beginnings as a weary guitar chord progression. As Cave delivers the song in a grand, hazy style, which at times can only be described as a slurring drawl, the intensity gradually increases. The drums become more purposeful, the backing vocals more passionate, and wind and horn instruments give an immense power before the fierceness suddenly retreats and the song gently comes to a close. This song and 'Jubilee Street' are the strongest material on an album of exceptional quality.

'Push The Sky Away' (Cave, Ellis) (4:07)

The dominance of Ellis' synth playing on this track predicts the even stronger synth drive of the next two Bad Seeds albums – its slow and relentless dirge inspiring a sense of melancholy. This is incredibly sparse, with only minimal group support as Cave pleads with the listener to not give up:

> And if you feel you got everything you came for
> If you got everything and you don't want no more
> You've got to just keep on pushing
> Keep on pushing
> Push the sky away

Again, it's open to interpretation. The plea could be in regard to suicide, not giving in to complacency, or just trying to keep up with life as an ageing individual edging closer to the sky: or, in other words, closer to death. Whatever the meaning, it's a haunting closer, made all the more spectral by the choir of children who join in on the later refrain.

Skeleton Tree (2016)

Personnel:
Nick cave: vocals, piano, Wurlitzer, synthesizer, vibes, backing vocals
Warren Ellis: synthesizer, loops, Wurlitzer, piano, baritone tenor guitar, violin, viola, drum treatments, drum loops, backing vocals
Martyn P. Casey: bass
Jim Sclavunos: percussion, vibes, tubular bells, backing vocals
George Vjestica: acoustic guitar, backing vocals
Thomas Wydler: drums
Guest musicians:
Else Torp: additional vocals ('Distant Sky')
Ellie Wyatt: violin
Charlotte Glasson: viola
Joe Giddey: cello
Recorded at The Retreat, Brighton; La Frette, La-Frette-sur-Seine, France; Air Studios, London, 2014-2016
Producers: Nick Cave, Warren Ellis, Nick Launay
Label: Bad Seed Ltd.
Release date: 9 September 2016
Chart positions: UK: 2, USA: 27, Australia: 1
Running time: 39:42

Death has always been one of Cave's recurring themes – indeed, we've thus far come across a plethora of characters who have lost their lives in the most brutal ways. Cave is also no stranger to grief, having been deeply affected in his youth by his father's death in a car accident. Cave also lost his friend and Birthday Party bandmate Tracy Pew, who died after hitting his head on a bathtub during a seizure. But Cave was about to be confronted with another death that he wasn't the author of: a personal tragedy that every parent hopes to never have to navigate.

Much of the recording for the band's 16th studio album had already been completed at Brighton's The Retreat, with a view to finishing it off in Paris later. But in 2015, the unthinkable happened – Cave and Susie's 15-year-old son Arthur Cave died after accidentally falling off a cliff as a result of experimenting with LSD for the first time – a trauma that had a huge effect on the album's completion and its overall spirit as detailed in a 2017 interview for *The Australian*: 'The truth of it, is that there is not a note or word on the album that is not affected by Arthur's death', exclaimed Cave a few months after the album's release.

Despite the devastating effect of this tragedy, Cave and the band did resume work on the album as planned, but in the initial aftermath of such an event, returning to work was difficult – Cave later describing it as 'terrifying' but also 'important': 'I was a mess, big time. So was everybody, actually'. Furthermore, the recording process in Paris proved to be tricky in terms of polishing the tracks recorded in Brighton. According to Cave in the same interview, finessing the tracks failed to elevate them: 'The record itself in its untreated state was simply refusing to allow itself to be embellished or polished'. And at the time of release, the album was noted for its less-polished production. Not that this is a detriment to the album – rather, it adds to the pervading sense of weariness; Cave's voice sounding particularly fragile and exhausted.

Musically, *Skeleton Tree* is the natural follow-up to *Push the Sky Away*, with the drive of synthesizers being more emphasised here, and ambient textures featuring more heavily. But if its predecessor boasted extended epics like 'Jubilee Street' and 'Higgs Boson Blues', the songs here are so fragile that you almost have to question whether they aren't already broken to an extent. The band somehow become even more stripped back, relying more on Ellis' loops, pulses, sound treatments and captivating string arrangements, while the guitar is phased out further, and Cave's piano makes a return. Many describe the sound as avant-garde due to the adoption of musical dissonance, free-form structure and rhythmical ambiguity – think Scott Walker if you want a comparison.

Meanwhile, lyrically, Cave had become further disenchanted with the narrative style as he asserted in *One More Time with Feeling*: 'I don't actually believe that is what life is like: that there is a pleasing narrative'. Indeed, the stream-of-consciousness that Cave adopted on *Push* is intensified here, to the point that there's no clear storyline anywhere. Instead, thoughts and ideas are jumbled together, and function allegorically. Cave even improvised some of the lyrics, reflecting the chaotic thoughts of someone in the throes of immediate grief: 'Because the lyrics are essentially improvised, they tend to be ambiguous, unguarded, and to a certain extent, beyond my control. This, I believe, gives these particular songs their reckless power' (*Red Hand Files* issue #56). However, it's important to remember that most of the material was composed and recorded before Arthur's death – though, in the aftermath, Cave amended some of the lyrics to reflect ensuing events, strengthening Arthur's bond to the album.

In order to avoid the laborious and painful task of going over such trauma in countless interviews, Cave commissioned Andrew Dominik to create a documentary film that would answer all the possible questions Cave wanted to avoid answering in person. The accompanying film *One More Time with Feeling* documents the album's completion. And just as Arthur looms over the album itself, so too is his presence felt on Dominik's compelling companion to the album, albeit Arthur is never directly mentioned. As wonderful as it is to see these songs being performed in the studio – and to gain insight into the Cave/Ellis partnership and the creative process overall – it's heartbreaking to see Cave wrestling with his grief. The whole film is presented in black and white – an apt filter for a mournful sound – something that's also reflected in the album's minimalist black cover.

Both the album and its accompanying film were lauded on release, and for good reason. From start to finish, it's an entrancing listen; beautiful and devastating, as Cave navigates his way through the immediacy of his grief, presenting his untethered thoughts over the Bad Seeds' sorrowfully-ambient meanderings. This would be my favourite Bad Seeds album, along with *The Boatman's Call*, if it wasn't for the album that came next: an album that deals with a grief more considered.

'Jesus Alone' (Cave, Ellis) (5:52)

We open with ominous vibrations that almost sound animalistic, along with the random, gentle patter of Wydler's drum kit, and an uneasy string section that rises and falls incrementally. Ellis' haunting soundscapes add to the overall eeriness of a track that immediately brings Arthur into focus – 'You fell from the sky/Crash landed in a field/Near the river Adur': bravely direct opening lines. Over the track, we're presented with images conjuring different emotions that one may circle around in the immediacy of grief. Happiness – provided perhaps by memories of a lost loved one – is evoked in the lines 'You're a woman in a yellow dress/Surrounded by a charm of hummingbirds'. Whereas 'You're a drug addict lying on your back/In a Tijuana hotel room' conveys a feeling of exhaustion and entrapment. My favourite line in the song is 'You're an African doctor harvesting tear ducts'. The idea of being able to eradicate grief by removing the organs responsible for such an emotional response is an interesting one, and perhaps desirable for someone in such unimaginable pain. Cave's piano introduces brief moments of stability in the refrain, in which Cave declares, 'With my voice, I am calling you' – a calling from the material world, directed at his son in the spiritual realm, wherever that may be. Or maybe it's a cry directed at those listeners who may also be in the throes of immediate grief: a gathering of mutual bereavement.

'Rings Of Saturn' (Cave, Ellis) (3:28)

We move to something a little lighter, brighter and floaty, propelled by a steady filtered drum rhythm. Synthesizer is prominent here, the main chord progression outlined by a syrupy soundscape, made all the sweeter by high-pitched chirps. The piano joins in from the first refrain, which changes meaning after each verse: 'And this is the moment/This is exactly where she is born to be/Now this is what she does and this is what she is'. The first verse seems to outline a sexual encounter with the woman in question, made clear through multiple sexual images: 'black oily gash', 'on all eights', 'like a 'funnel-web'. The proceeding refrain seems rather one-dimensional in that all it suggests is she's meant to be there in the moment. The second verse is a little more complicated, as the narrator struggles to comprehend the woman, as he 'spurts his ink across the sheets' and leaves her 'completely unexplained'. The following refrain now declares such inconceivability, suggesting she's this unimaginable force that can't be explained. The final verse reveals her to be a mother, 'Stepping over heaps of sleeping children', and by the end, she ascends and 'dangles herself like a child's dream from the rings of Saturn'. In the mind of a child, she is their holy protector from above, who can make dreams come true.

'Girl In Amber' (Cave, Ellis) (4:51)

This is one of the album's most affecting pieces of music: a ballad that radiates unshakable grief. Amid a cascade of gentle synths and quivering string interjections, Cave sounds at his most fragile, croaky and exhausted as he sings above a sombre, funereal piano part. The song title was conceived when recording in Brighton after Cave found inspiration from a paperweight with a spider trapped inside it. After the tragedy, the song took on a deeper meaning, and it became clear who Cave's girl in amber was as he explains in issue #85 of *The Red Hand Files*:

> It was suddenly and tragically clear that 'Girl in Amber' had found its 'who'. The 'who' was Susie, my wife – held impossibly, as she was at the time, within her grief, reliving each day a relentless spinning song that began with the ringing of the phone and ended with the collapse of her world.

Cave reflects on how much grief can entrap – in this case, the amber being the grief that stops Susie from breaking free and moving forward. The idea of being stuck in an endless cycle is clear in the lines 'The song, the song it spins/It spins now since 1984' – not just in terms of the album-tour-album-tour rigmarole, but in the construction of the line: stuck on the same word as if the whole system is broken. But the tears really start to flow when you hear lines that so clearly reference Arthur: 'You kneel, lace up his shoes/Your little blue-eyed boy'. The final repeated line 'Don't touch me' was an addition after the tragedy had occurred – a harrowing final wish hinting at the fragility of grief, as if any sort of reassuring embrace would be too much to handle. This stands as one of Cave's most brutal ballads.

'Magneto' (Cave, Ellis) (5:22)

Contrary to the opinion of many fans, this is the album highlight for me. It's unsettling, it's restless, it's hushed and exhausted, but most of all, it sounds like an old machine struggling to power up – but stuttering and gasping, it fails. It's untethered by a clear rhythm section, moving fluidly through the hopeless gloom, tired and reluctant. Everything is fragmented, including the lyrics, which transition from images of mundane activities that become so difficult to cope with that they inspire violence ('Oh, the urge to kill somebody was basically overwhelming/I had such hard blues down there in the supermarket queues'), to harrowing depictions of the physical assault grief enacts on the body ('I was an electrical storm on the bathroom floor, clutching the bowl/My blood was full of gags and other people's diseases'). I like the idea that grief is akin to having 'other people's diseases', highlighting grief's debilitating effects. The refrain line 'And one more time with feeling' that Cave circles back to – which is where the title for Dominik's film comes from – feels like Cave is attempting over and over again to make sense of this tragedy, but ultimately it doesn't make sense: the disjointed accompaniment reflecting these broken, desperate attempts to find meaning.

'Anthrocene' (Cave, Ellis) (4:34)

In many ways, this is similar to the previous track but is less gloomy and a little more jazz-like. Everything is still very much disjointed, and there's no stable bedrock, only Wydler's furious drum scurries, which really stand out. Once again, amid pulsing synthesizer waves and wearied background coos, Cave babbles in a stream of consciousness. The title is a shortened variant of the geological epoch Anthropocene. The natural world outlined here is dying under the hammer of humanity's activities: 'Flowers fall to their naked knees', 'The dark force that shifts at the edge of the trees', 'Behold, behold, the Heaven-bound seas'. But there seems to be a parallel in which nature's loss of life and colour is mirrored within Cave – much like nature is ravaged in the age of anthrocene, he is being ravaged in an age of grief. And so it is in lines such as 'Oh the things we love, we love, we love, we lose', that this parallel can be seen. It simultaneously highlights our dependency on the stability of Earth's environment to keep those that we love while also being a more personal lyric referencing the loss of Cave's beloved son.

'I Need You' (Cave, Ellis) (5:58)

At first glance, this lyric would fit on *The Boatman's Call*, with lines like 'I saw you standing there in the supermarket/With your red dress falling and your eyes are to the ground' and 'I will miss you when you're gone/I'll miss you when you're gone away forever'. But in the context of this record, Cave pleads with his lover to not drown in the painful waters of grief as she struggles to stay afloat. But everything seems to be 'falling' – her hair 'hanging down', her dress 'falling' and her eyes 'to the ground'. As she falls further into a pit of misery, she's slipping away from him. However, there is a sense of hope in the uplifting musical accompaniment, which feels a lot more stable and certain in its convention. It could almost be called synth-pop, powered by rich, warm lashings of synth, which, along with the more energised vocal, give the track a fullness that the others don't have.

'Distant Sky' (Cave, Ellis) (5:36)

This may just be the most beautiful yet fragile track on the record. We move from the boldest to the most weightless track on the album, characterised by feathery organ-like synths, restrained strings and incredibly minimal percussion. Cave is joined by Danish singer Else Torp, whose tender, angelic soprano voice only adds to the fragility as they sing about escaping the mortal world to a spiritual one in the skies:

Let us go now, my one true love
Call the gasman, cut the power out
We can set out, we can set out for the distant skies
Watch the sun, watch it rising in your eyes

Perhaps this is to escape Cave's emotional mortal world turmoil, or to be closer to his son in the spiritual world. But undeniably, the most crushing lines are 'They told us our dreams would outlive us/They told us our gods would outlive us/But they lied'. To me, this is about Arthur – the person Cave worships and fulfils his dreams through; his child that was supposed to outlive his parents. There is despair in the delivery of 'but they lied'. It's a tearjerker, but for all the sadness it evokes, the image of children climbing up to the sun is elevating, and it's an image that Cave continued to explore on the next record.

'Skeleton Tree' (Cave, Ellis) (4:01)
Some call the closing track cathartic, but I'm not so sure. Maybe in some ways it is. There is the awareness that 'nothing is for free' – that with strong love comes debilitating grief when faced with loss. Towards the end, Cave repeats, 'And it's alright now' – an acceptance, but one that doesn't feel reassuring at all. He's still in the depths of his grief; the very image of a skeleton tree suggesting emptiness and lifelessness. Furthermore, Cave is still isolated from the world around him; the 'jittery TV glowing white like fire' bringing to mind TV static; Cave being trapped in a sort of stasis, cut off from the world. When he calls out across the sea overlooking his home, 'the echo comes back empty'. His attempts to call his son back to life suggest Cave hasn't yet fully accepted the situation. But this is not to say he never will – the accompaniment being a more languid version of 'I Need You', but still optimistic. Warm synth, acoustic guitar and a steady rhythm section pave the way towards recovery, while the backing chorus on those final lines highlight how Cave is not alone and, in time, it will be 'alright now'.

Ghosteen (2019)

Personnel:
Nick Cave: vocals, piano, synthesizer, backing vocals
Warren Ellis: synthesizer, loops, flute, violin, piano, backing vocals
Martyn P. Casey: bass
Jim Sclavunos: vibraphone, percussion
George Vjestica: guitar
Thomas Wydler: drums
Guest musicians:
Augustin Viard: ondes martenot
Kaushlesh 'Garry' Purohit: tabla
Ben Foster: string arrangement, conducting
Sam Thompson: string arrangement assistance
Tom Pigott-Smith: leading
Steve Morris: leading of seconds
Bruce White: first viola
Nick Cooper: first cello
Mary Scully: first double bass
Recorded at Woodshed Studios, Malibu; NightBird Studios, Hollywood; The Retreat, Brighton; Candy Bomber, Berlin; Air Studios, London, 2018-2019
Producers: Nick Cave, Warren Ellis
Label: Bad Seed Ltd.
Release date: 4 October 2019
Chart positions: UK: 4, USA: 108, Australia: 2
Running time: 68:10

In One More Time with Feeling, there is a line from Cave that rings true when we come to consider the Bad Seeds' latest album: 'Time is elastic. We can go away from the event, but at some point, the elastic snaps and we always come back to it': what a great analogy. If *Skeleton Tree* represented grief in its immediacy, the next album is the product of an ongoing healing process – a grief that still very much exists but is more measured.

Part of Cave's healing process was his effort to engage with his audience on a more intimate level. In 2018 he embarked on a limited Q&A tour called Conversations with Nick. It was a therapy session of sorts, where he answered questions from fans and treated them to piano-only versions of their song requests. But perhaps the most significant gateway between artist and fan was the creation of The Red Hand Files later that year, an online platform with one simple function: 'You can ask me anything. There will be no moderator. This will be between you and me. Let's see what happens'. You can only do three things on the site – ask a question, subscribe to receive Cave's latest responses, and peruse past responses. The topics are far-ranging, but much of the dialogue revolves around philosophical questions, and of course, there are moments in which Arthur is mentioned.

But in 2019, there was one post on The Red Hand Files that sparked excitement within the fan base – in response to a question regarding the likelihood of a new album, Cave responded in issue #63 with this: 'You can expect a new album next week. It is called *Ghosteen*. It is a double album. The songs on the first album are the children. The songs on the second are their parents. Ghosteen is a migrating spirit. Love, Nick'. This was going to be the first Cave album I would experience listening to and buying upon release as a Cave fan. So you can imagine how excited I was. I remember going out and buying *Ghosteen* on vinyl, listening for the first time in the evening with all the lights dimmed in my student house, and just being overwhelmed throughout. It is the next natural step beyond *Skeleton Tree*. It's the final album in a trilogy that's been reliant on synthesizers, loops, orchestration and ambient soundscapes. But here, there's further reliance on those. There's not a guitar in sight, and the piano appears infrequently. But the most noticeable absence is Wydler's percussion which ended up being mostly removed from the final mix. When asked about this, Cave responded in issue #73 of *The Red Hand Files*: 'Thomas Wydler, our drummer, did some amazing work on this record. However, after a great deal of thought, we all felt that the drums anchored the songs to the ground and didn't allow them to float. The decision was not made lightly or on a whim. Rather it was a tough artistic decision determined by the needs of the songs themselves'.

Indeed, on *Skeleton Tree,* there were occasional moments when the songs felt incredibly weighed down and gloomy (which is not a bad thing) due to rumbling synths and grounding percussion. But 'Distant Sky' paved the way for the airy, floating sounds of *Ghosteen*. This makes a great deal of sense – *Skeleton Tree* is mainly grounded in the material world, except for 'Distant Sky', which attempts to escape into the spiritual realm where *Ghosteen* mainly takes place: 'We wanted each song to feel as if it were climbing toward an exultant and euphoric state; for the record to be a vessel that transported the listener far away from the world and its troubles, and that it lived in the jubilant and hopeful beyond' (issue #73). This is what the lyrics were aspiring to do – to heal Cave's grief in the material world by connecting with his son in the spiritual, wherever that may be. The words have a metaphysical edge and something much more communal compared to those on *Skeleton Tree*, which mainly focused on Cave's own grief. Here, he brings onboard the other trauma sufferers in the same healing process and guides himself and everyone else to a place of comfort and assurance. The artwork – available on The Red Hand Files prior to the album release – is indicative of such a place: a Garden of Eden-type destination shown on a cover that radiates optimism and hope.

On release, the album was unsurprisingly hailed as a masterpiece. Co-writer Warren Ellis cites the album as the greatest artistic achievement he's been a part of in a 2021 *Stereogum* interview: 'I don't think I could ever be involved in anything this great again. I always thought one day my aim is to make something great, and it felt like that happened'. Ellis thought it was so great that it would be his final collaboration with Cave. But the release of *Carnage* in 2021 – an album credited to just Cave and Ellis – obviously negated such a thought.

As of now, there doesn't appear to be any new activity from the Bad Seeds, as Cave and Ellis will continue riding the wave of *Ghosteen* and *Carnage* through a new documentary film directed by Andrew Dominik, titled *This Much I Know to be True*: a companion piece to *One More Time with Feeling*. This doesn't bother me – *Ghosteen* stands as one of the band's greatest achievements, and it should be milked for all it's worth.

The Children
'Spinning Song' (Cave, Ellis) (4:43)
We are instantly encapsulated in Ellis' swirling synthesizers, which are warm, inviting and wrap around you like a reassuring embrace. Cave begins with the lines, 'Once there was a song/A song that yearned to be sung' – lines that define his career, as it's a song that has been 'spinning now since 1984', as Cave asserted in 'Girl in Amber'. The common reading of this lyric places Elvis as 'the king of rock 'n' roll' with his 'black jelly hair'. The queen – his wife – plants a tree:

> The garden tree was a stairway, it was sixteen branches high
> On the top branch was a nest, sing the high cloudy nest
> In the nest there was a bird, the bird had a wing
> The wing had a feather, spin the feather and sing the wind

When the king dies, the queen is heartbroken and the tree retreats into the earth along with the nest and the bird. But the feather – a symbol of Elvis' musical legacy – continues to spin 'upward and upward and upward/Spinning all the weather vanes'. But I prefer to read this as a mythical story that's more personal to Cave, in which he and Susie plant a tree that springs forth a mythical world of spirit children and galleon ships, that we will encounter later. In the immediacy of Arthur's death, these fantastical hopes and dreams all collapse, and reality sets in: 'And you're sitting at the kitchen table, listening to the radio'. This whole album is about trying to regain these lost hopes and dreams, and in this track's final euphoric moments, a rising angelic choir and powerful organ, elevate the concluding lines of reassurance – atypically delivered in falsetto: 'Peace will come, and peace will come, and peace will come in time/Time will come, and time will come, a time will come for us'. This glorious opening track sets up everything to come.

'Bright Horses' (Cave, Ellis) (4:52)
This is a piano-driven ballad, with synth providing a lush backdrop along with subtle vibraphone, Ellis' backing howls and languid string interjections. The first verse continues the previous track's mythic undertones: Cave conjuring

images of bright, flaming 'horses of love/Their manes full of fire'. But in the second verse, the cold, hard reality of life hits home:

We're all so sick and tired of seeing things as they are
Horses are just horses and their manes aren't full of fire

And there's no shortage of tyrants, and no shortage of fools
And the little white shape dancing at the end of the hall

But that 'little white shape' is Ghosteen – the album's migrating spirit; Arthur reanimated in spirit form, giving Cave the confidence to 'believe in something', despite the cruel reality of life. 'But my baby's coming home now, on the 5:30 train' he sings optimistically in the final verse – devoid of synth, and now coated in rich, full-bodied strings. It doesn't matter that Arthur can't be met in his mortal form – his spirit can visit Cave, even 'on the 5:30 train'.

'Waiting For You' (Cave, Ellis) (3:54)
Beginning with an industrial pulse that fades as the piano enters, this is a similar ballad style to the previous track, albeit more sparse. Synths again provide gentle support, but Cave's voice is really allowed to shine on this stripped-back track. It mirrors the calm of a nighttime drive that Cave and his wife embark on here, parking on 'the beach in the cool, evening air'. Much like the track's open space, there is a silence between the couple that doesn't need to be filled with words: 'Well, sometimes it's better not to say anything at all'. But grieving has many forms – for Susie, facing the hard reality head-on is her preference; her 'body is an anchor, never asked to be free', whereas Cave relies on faith to bring some sort of phenomenon that will cure his grief: 'A Jesus freak on the street says He is returning/Well sometimes a little bit of faith can go a long, long way'. This doesn't cause a rift, as Cave tells her to 'take as long as you need', finally declaring, 'I'm just waiting for you... to return' – to return to him from the depths of her grief.

'Night Raid' (Cave, Ellis) (5:07)
Propelled by synthesized church bells above a bed of more synth, the action takes place in room 33 of the Grand Hotel. I was wracking my brain trying to decipher the meaning of the lyrics, and I believe they detail the conception of Cave and Susie's twins. Sexual undertones can be gleaned from the lines 'the spurting font of creativity' and 'I slid my little songs out from under you' – the latter being a line that migrated from one song to another, finally finding its place here. Then there's the biological detail that includes the title: 'They were runaway flakes of snow, yeah, I know/They annexed your insides in a late-night raid'. But again, in a world of humming cars and pouring rain, Cave chooses to believe in something greater: 'And we all rose up from our

wonder/We will never admit defeat'. The twins' conception then takes place in an elevated room, where this otherness exists separate from the reality of the world outside.

'Sun Forest' (Cave, Ellis) (6:46)

It's hard to describe how beautiful this track is – it, along with 'Spinning Song', being the album highlight. A two-minute ambient synth introduction aptly communicates the beauty of Cave's surroundings:

> I lay in the forest amongst the butterflies and the fireflies
> And the burning horses and the flaming trees
> As a spiral of children climb up to the sun
> Waving goodbye to you and goodbye to me

It's some of his most dream-like poetry, as he places himself in the spiritual world portrayed on the album cover. Cave puts his grief behind him – characterised by lines like 'To be standing here alone with nowhere to be/ With a man mad with grief and on each side a thief/Everybody hanging from a tree, from a tree' – as he waves 'goodbye to all that as the future rolls in'. It's a future made euphoric and jubilant in the chorus: the album's most beautiful musical moment. An angelic chorus of backing vocals in a glorious wash of strings and synths, elevate the majestic imagery: 'A spiral of children climbs up to the sun, to the sun, to the sun/And on each golden rung, a spiral of children climbs up to the sun'. It's a breathtaking moment that appears twice in the song, before the coda, which fades in like a feather on the wind. We then hear the voice of Ghosteen, represented by Cave's falsetto: 'I am here beside you/ Look for me in the sun/I am beside you, I am within/In the sunshine, in the sun'. His callings on 'Skeleton Tree' no longer come back empty as he connects with the spiritual reanimation of his son.

'Galleon Ship' (Cave, Ellis) (4:14)

Here Cave will make that same journey to the sun, but in a galleon ship, initially believing himself to be 'a long, lonely rider across the sky'. But later, after a glorious instrumental middle section of distant ghostly backing howls and intense synths that gently rise and fall incrementally, Cave realises there are others embarking upon the same journey through grief: 'For we are not alone, it seems/So many riders in the sky/The winds of longing in their sails/ Searching for the other side'. The lines of communication Cave opened up through the creation of The Red Hand Files, have manifested themselves here, as he realises that grief has also affected his fans at some point. Here, Cave is joined by those people in their mutual quest to find some sort of peace, represented by those haunting multiple intersecting voices. The lilt of this synth-driven piece reflects the journey's bumpy ride for all of those hoping to eventually arrive.

'Ghosteen Speaks' (Cave, Ellis) (4:02)

Everything feels a little calmer, less intense and more relaxed in comparison to the previous two tracks. Whirling synths, reassuring bass tones and bright backing vocals give this a heavenly quality, as we again hear from Ghosteen: 'I am beside you/Look for me'. The communal spirit of grief is made clear in lines such as, 'I think they're singing to be free/I think my friends have gathered here for me'. Ghosteen is not only a spirit that can be interpreted as a reanimation of Arthur but it is also a much bigger entity – a shape-shifting reanimation of lost loved ones far and wide, or perhaps some sort of inner god. Whatever it is, it's there to help everyone desiring freedom from grief: the choral vocals representing the multiple voices directing their pain towards Ghosteen, and 'singing to be free'.

'Leviathan' (Cave, Ellis) (4:47)

Here Cave returns to the beach with his wife to say only one thing, like a sort of incantation: 'Oh my, oh my, oh my, oh my/I love my baby and my baby loves me'. Piano, synths, and in the distant background gentle hand drums, make up the bulk of this track, initially quiet and understated. But on each repetition of Cave's mantra, the intensity grows towards a majestic climax of heavenly organ tones and layered backing vocals, creating a soundscape that I believe you would hear at the gates of paradise. This beautiful ending comes 'as the sun sinks into the water now' – a blackening that suggests we're not finished. Indeed, there is more to come as we next hear the parent tracks.

Their Parents
'Ghosteen' (Cave, Ellis) (12:10)

This first extended parent track opens rather ominously before quickly unfurling into a cinematic delight of strings and synthesizer repeating a melody of great magnitude, becoming even more grandiose with each cycle. Not until the four-minute mark do we hear Cave, who begins optimistically: 'This world is beautiful/Held within its stars/I keep it in my heart'. Then there's a transition into a major key, and the soundscape becomes even fuller, with piano, elevating backing vocals, soaring strings and an ambient, subtle drum groove. In this joyous section, Ghosteen is celebrated in all its glory: 'A ghosteen dances in my hand/Slowly twirling, twirling all around/Glowing circle in my hand'. Like a ballerina, Ghosteen is graceful and elegant; a glowing beacon of hope in the dark. 'Slowly twirling' makes me think of the rotating figure in a musical box, which speaks of the album's ability to make you dream like you once did as a child with a wild imagination.

Then Cave signals the retreat of this optimism with three words: 'Here we go': a preparation for the sombre second half. Everything is sucked out of this next section, leaving just a synth in the low register, and occasional mournful backing-vocal whimpers. The infantile undertones mentioned earlier return through a retelling of Cave's situation in the context of a children's story: 'Mama bear holds the remote/Papa bear he just floats/And baby bear, he has gone to the moon in a boat, on a boat'. Susie is grounded in reality, Cave 'floats' in a dream world, whilst Arthur has transitioned into the afterlife. I love that these are meant to be Cave's nighttime thoughts – the sparse accompaniment reflecting the stillness and the underlying sorrow. The personification of the Moon – a 'moonlit man' who moves down the road and 'kisses you lightly' and 'leaves your sleeping body', is so calming and tender – its light a reassurance despite the pain of knowing that 'the past with its fierce undertow won't ever let us go'. But this is not entirely melancholy, as Cave accepts he can still love his son without him physically being there: 'Well there's nothing wrong with loving things that cannot even stand'. But Cave doesn't want to stay up all night talking to the Moony man, as he 'won't get a wink of sleep' otherwise. This entire section is such a beautiful moment of still reflection – both sections together communicating the simultaneous feeling of rejuvenated hope, joy and underlying grief that can creep up on you in moments of quiet.

'Fireflies' (Cave, Ellis) (3:23)

The words to this narrated piece of music were the first from the album to be seen by fans, as they were posted on The Red Hand Files a year before the album's release. Behind an unsettling backdrop of jittering strings, pulsing low-register piano notes and distant ghostly voices, Cave makes clear the banality of our existence: 'We are photons released from a dying star/We are fireflies a child has trapped in a jar' – the child perhaps representing God. In saying we are fireflies trapped in a jar, Cave suggests we are meaningless and insignificant and cannot escape our existence. He sides with predictable rationale over the power of the imagination that has driven so much of this album – although the sky being 'full of momentary light' perhaps represents moments of creative inspiration that help to alleviate such a bleak, predictable existence. But it's the repeated line at the end of each stanza that's the most significant: 'We are here, and you are where you are'.

There's a kind of relief in the fact that Arthur is no longer trapped in such a bleak existence where 'there is no order'. Instead, he is elsewhere. But Cave doesn't attempt the inconceivable task of trying to label such an afterlife, and doesn't claim to know of such a place either. There is an acceptance here – one that's anchored in reality but still open to the possibility of an afterlife, whatever that may be.

'Hollywood' (Cave, Ellis) (14:12)

And so we come to the final track – some of its evocative images being the first that influenced the rest of the album's writing. Unlike on the title track, a bass loop propels this extended song throughout, musically resisting any radical change. This is also arguably the album's heaviest and most ominous track; its rumble bringing to mind moments from *Skeleton Tree*, albeit there's an effort to end optimistically. Wydler's drum kit makes another appearance here, for a longer duration, though his steady groove is still not as up-front.

Over the bass loop's relentless course, Cave regurgitates a series of disparate images, beginning with him driving to a Malibu ravaged in flames: 'The fires continued through the night', 'I'm gonna buy me a house up in the hills/ With a tear-shaped pool and a gun that kills'. We are brought back to reality: a reality that's collapsing before Cave's eyes as a result of his grief. There is much anger and hatred in the first half: Cave's wife described as a cougar who roams Malibu 'with a terrible engine of wrath for a heart'. These grief-stricken images moored in reality, conflict with those in Cave's imagination that have driven so much of this album:

Now I'm standing on the shore
All the animals roam the beaches
Sea creatures rise out of the sea
And I'm standing on the shore
Everyone begins to run
The kid drops his bucket and spade and climbs into the sun

In the midst of animals retreating from the fires to the shore and people running away in fear, we have mythical creatures rising from the sea and the image of a child climbing towards the sun, an image that has been central to this album. In this state of conflict between the real and the imaginary, Cave does not despair but simply states, 'And I'm just waiting now, for peace to come'. Even though it may not seem it, he knows that one day the conflict he finds himself in will resolve and he will be granted peace.

The final image is perhaps his greatest assertion of acceptance: delivered entirely in falsetto. Cave retells the Buddhist story of Kisa and the mustard seed. In order to cure her dying baby, Kisa is told she must collect a mustard seed from every household that has not at some point been touched by death. But she finds no such household, as everyone has experienced losing a loved one at least once, and she concludes that 'Everybody's losing someone'. Through the mustard seed story, Cave again acknowledges he's not alone in his grief; that anyone could be experiencing the same tumultuous journey. Even though this may be of some comfort to him, in his final lines, he admits that 'It's a long way to find peace of mind', 'And I'm just waiting now, for peace to come, for peace to come'. The closing tracks to this album and *Skeleton Tree* are similar in that they end on a note of uncertainty. But there's also a huge difference – Cave accepts he's still grieving and that it's a long road, but there is optimism in the fact that he knows he will one day find peace of mind: not cured of his grief, but just simply at peace.

Live Albums
Live Seeds (1993)
Personnel:
Nick Cave: vocals, organ, piano
Mick Harvey: guitar, xylophone, backing vocals
Blixa Bargeld: guitar, backing vocals
Martyn P. Casey: bass, backing vocals
Conway Savage: piano, organ, backing vocals
Thomas Wydler: drums
Additional musicians:
The Cruel Sea: backing vocals
Recorded at various concerts in Europe and Australia, 1992-1993
Producers: The Bad Seeds
Label: Mute Records
Release date: 28 September 1993
Chart positions: UK: 67, USA: -, Australia: 47
Running time: 60:35

After the band's debacle with producer David Briggs during the recording of
Henry's Dream, Cave and Harvey were left disappointed by an initial mix that
failed to provide the abrasive, brash punch of the acoustic 'trash can' songs that
had enamoured Cave when encountering buskers on the streets of Brazil. The
original mix was so inadequate that Cave and Harvey enlisted Tony Cohen to
remix the album. But even this was not enough to satisfy the duo.

To make up for this travesty, the *Live Seeds* album presented tracks from
the album in the way that was originally intended: with a raw and unpolished
snarl. They were recorded at various venues on the 1992-1993 *Henry's Dream*
tour, with four tracks from that album included: 'Papa Won't Leave You Henry',
'John Finn's Wife', 'Brother, My Cup Is Empty' and 'Jack The Ripper'. The other
eight are live renditions of past material, including 'The Mercy Seat', 'From Her
To Eternity' and 'Tupelo'. There's also a track called 'Plain Gold Ring' – a cover
of a Nina Simone song that the band had not included on an album previously.

But it's the live renditions of songs from *Henry's Dream* that are to be
scrutinised against their studio companions. Some fans believe these live
versions greatly surpass the studio efforts, and there's a visceral energy and a
punch on the *Live Seeds* versions. But other fans can't really tell the difference,
and I'm more inclined to place myself in that camp. Though the live versions
are superb, I personally don't have any qualm with the studio versions: I
believe both hold up. The *Live Seeds* album is an excellent live album debut,
showcasing the strength of a wide-ranging back-catalogue.

The Abattoir Blues Tour (2007)
Personnel:
Nick cave: vocals, piano

Mick Harvey: guitars, bouzouki
Warren Ellis: violin, mandolin, bouzouki, flute
James Johnston: organ, guitar
Conway Savage: piano
Jim Sclavunos, Thomas Wydler: drums, percussion
Additional musicians:
Geo Onaymake, Eleanor Palmer, Wendi Rose: background vocals
Chris Bailey: guest vocals ('Bring It On')
Blixa Bargeld: features in the 'Bring It On' and 'Babe, I'm On Fire' videos
Recorded at various concerts in Europe, 2003-2004
Producers: Chris Thompson, Mick Harvey
Label: Mute Records
Release date: 29 January 2007
Chart positions: UK: -, USA: -
Running time: 91:46

It was ten years before another live Bad Seeds album, this second release being the live companion to their grandiose 2004 double album *Abattoir/Lyre*. The *Abattoir Blues Tour* was released as a double-CD/double-DVD set. The 17 tracks on the CDs were assembled from different shows from the European tour. Songs from *Abattoir/Lyre* make up the bulk of the set, which is no surprise considering Cave was then enthused with the new direction the band had taken after the departure of Blixa Bargeld. But some tracks are from an era gone by – 'Red Right Hand', 'Stagger Lee', 'Deanna' and 'The Ship Song' sit alongside the main stars of the show.

The double-DVD set presents a separate show on each disc. The first disc has a 2004 Brixton Hall Academy show; the second, a 2003 show at the London Hammersmith Apollo before the release of *Abattoir/Lyre*. The Brixton Hall set is similar to the CD set, but because it's taken from one continuous show, the flow is better. The Hammersmith show offers seven tracks of earlier material, including 'Christina The Astonishing', 'Sad Waters', 'Nobody's Baby Now' and some from *Nocturama*. This second DVD also includes bonus material, such as promotional videos for songs from both *Abattoir/Lyre* and *Nocturama*, and a short film about *Abattoir/Lyre*. Overall, this live release is much more expansive than the previous one: a comprehensive melding of the old with the new.

Live at the Royal Albert Hall (2008)

Personnel:
Nick Cave: vocals
Mick Harvey: guitars, organ, vibraphone
Blixa Bargeld: guitars, vocals
Martyn P. Casey: bass
Warren Ellis: violin
Conway Savage: piano, organ

Jim Sclavunos: percussion
Thomas Wydler: drums
Recorded at The Royal Albert Hall, London, 19/20 May 1997
Producers: Victor Van Vugt, Mick Harvey
Label: Mute Records
Release date: 24 November 2008
Chart positions: UK: -, US: -
Running time: 56:37

This third live album – released in 2008 – actually dates from the 1997 tour promoting *The Boatman's Call*. Of the 12, eight were originally released on a bonus nine-track CD included with the special edition of the band's first compilation album *The Best of Nick Cave & The Bad Seeds,* but in 2008 the bonus CD was released as a regular disc with four extra tracks. Unsurprisingly, many of the songs are taken from *The Boatman's Call* and other back-catalogue inclusions such as 'The Ship Song', 'Stranger Than Kindness' and 'Where The Wild Roses Grow' (which sees Blixa Bargeld take on Kylie Minogue's role) were in keeping with the band's more-mellow, reflective side that Cave was to continue to pursuing on *No More Shall We Part*. Perhaps this album's only anomaly is the final track: a rendition of 'The Mercy Seat' in all its thrashing, frenzied glory.

Live From KCRW (2013)

Personnel:
Nick Cave: vocals, piano
Warren Ellis: tenor guitar, violin, piano, loops, backing vocals
Barry Adamson: organ, percussion, backing vocals
Martyn P. Casey: bass
Jim Sclavunos: percussion, drums, backing vocals
Recorded at Apogee Studio, California, 18 April 2013
Producer: Bob Clearmountain
Label: Bad Seed Ltd.
Release date: 29 November 2013
Chart positions: UK: 81, USA: -
Running time: 52:15

The mood is mellower still on the band's fourth live album: recorded just after the release of *Push the Sky Away*. The ten tracks were performed by a stripped-back Bad Seeds lineup in a live session for the Santa Monica, California radio station KCRW. Four tracks from *Push* make up the bulk of this release, including the epic 'Higgs Boson Blues' and the hushed, synth-led 'Push The Sky Away'. Other back-catalogue goodies include moments from *The Boatman's Call* and *No More Shall We Part*, wildcard 'Jack The Ripper' and, of course, 'The Mercy Seat': albeit this version is more piano-driven, less frantic and therefore more revealing in its exposed state. Two extra tracks were included on the double-LP version: 'Into My Arms' and 'God Is In The House'.

Distant Sky: Live in Copenhagen (2018)

Personnel:
Nick Cave: vocals, piano
Warren Ellis: violin, tenor guitar, loops
Martyn P. Casey: bass
Larry Mullins: keyboards
Jim Sclavunos: tambourine, vibraphone, trigger pad, additional drums
George Vjestica: guitar
Thomas Wydler: drums
Additional musicians:
Else Torp: vocals ('Distant Sky')
Recorded at the Royal Arena, Copenhagen, 20 October 2017
Producers: Nick Cave, Warren Ellis
Label: Bad Seed Ltd.
Release date: 28 September 2018
Chart positions: UK: 74, US: -
Running time: 28:45

This is an EP consisting of only four tracks from a performance recorded after the release of *Skeleton Tree*. The EP came after the showing of David Barnard's concert film of the same name, which was made available for one night only in theatres, before being made available again on Cave's website for a brief period. Quality-over-quantity is the ethos here, with the opening rendition of 'Jubilee Street' being the best version I've ever heard of the song, reaching a euphoric climax. 'The Mercy Seat' and 'From Her To Eternity' are equally as charged and barbaric as you'd expect. But the beautiful rendition of 'Distant Sky' – featuring Danish soprano Else Torp reprising her angelic part from the studio version – defines this release.

Idiot Prayer: Nick Cave Alone at Alexandra Palace (2020)

Personnel:
Nick Cave: vocals, piano
Recorded at Alexandra Palace, London
Producers: Nick Cave, Dom Monks
Label: Bad Seed Ltd.
Release date: 20 November 2020
Chart positions: UK: 18, USA: -, Australia: 5
Running time: 83:53

Having been forced to cancel the upcoming *Ghosteen* tour, this live album was perhaps one of the most creative and imaginative responses to the COVID-19 pandemic and its debilitating effect on the live music scene. Here we have what the album title suggests: an isolated Cave buried in his mountains of notebooks and loose scraps of paper, at a piano in the middle of London's enormous Alexandra Palace. Originally, *Idiot Prayer* was put on sale as a live-streamed event taking place on 23 July, but later in the year, it was released as a concert film and live CD and double LP. As an extension of his Conversations with Nick tour, Cave performed 22 piano-only renditions of songs from the Bad Seeds catalogue, including a couple of Grinderman songs and the debut performance of a song called 'Euthanasia'. Of all Cave's live albums, this is the most vast and all-encompassing, with flavours of ten Bad Seeds albums contributing, though the bulk is naturally made up of songs from *The Boatman's Call*. It's captivating and haunting, and it exposes Cave's ambitious lyrics like never before. Instead of shunning away the effects of COVID, the album embraces the circumstances of its creation. The Disc 2 sleeve pictures an attendant in his mask, wiping down Cave's piano as he sits with his wife Susie standing over his shoulder. Cave's words on the back of the LP communicate such a refusal to hide the impact of COVID:

On 19th June 2020 – surrounded by COVID officers with tape measures and thermometers, masked-up gaffers and camera operators, nervous-looking technicians and buckets of hand gel – we created something very strange and very beautiful that spoke into this uncertain time but was in no way bowed by it ... a souvenir from a strange and precarious moment in history.

I was supposed to see Cave and the Bad Seeds on their upcoming tour (and I hope one day I will get to see them live), but this most pertinent release, quelled my disappointment.

Compilation Albums

The Best of Nick Cave & The Bad Seeds (1998)

This is the band's first compilation, stretching from their debut *From Her to Eternity* to the latest release at the time – *The Boatman's Call* – which was released one year prior. Before the compilation release, Cave asked each past and present band member to list some of their favourite tracks across their then ten albums. The results from this *would've* formed the bulk of the compilation. However, founding member Mick Harvey was the only member to respond to the request, so the track list is of Harvey's sole construction. Most of his choices are the major singles from each album: such as 'Red Right Hand', 'Into My Arms', 'The Mercy Seat' and 'Tupelo'. Oddly, these tracks are presented out of chronological order, which can be quite jarring. But overall, it stands as a solid representation of the band's highest moments up to *The Boatman's Call*.

B-sides & Rarities (2005)

This second compilation is a monster housing 56 tracks. Harvey compiled the 3-CD box set, incorporating what Cave calls 'forgotten songs' from across a 20-year career up until *Abattoir/Lyre*. For die-hard Cave fans, this is a goldmine of anything and everything that Harvey could find – acoustic versions and different interpretations of well-known Cave hits, along with B-sides and covers. It was reissued in 2021, along with a second part. Cave and Harvey posted a 30-minute conversation in which they talk about part one of the release. As well as enlightening fans as to some of their favourite tracks from part one, and explaining why they were relegated to B-side status, a lot of the conversation revolves around their relationship after Harvey's 2008 split from the band. Their public statement of friendship is refreshing to hear, and the stories they share and delight in recalling together, are rather amusing. As there are over 50 tracks, I won't go into as much detail with most of them – some are relatively self-explanatory.

'Deanna' (Acoustic Version) (2:51), 'The Mercy Seat' (Acoustic Version) (3:45) (Cave, Harvey), 'City of Refuge' (Acoustic Version) (2:42)

These are acoustic versions of songs from *Tender Prey* that were all included on a bonus 7" with initial pressings of *The Good Son* in 1990.

'The Moon Is In The Gutter' (2:35)

The down-tempo B-side of 'In the Ghetto' from the *From Her to Eternity* sessions is mainly piano-driven and is very bluesy in its communication of hopelessness: 'All my plans are flushed down the drain'.

'The Six Strings That Drew Blood' (4:47)

The B-side of 'Tupelo' from *The Firstborn is Dead*, this track is unsurprisingly bluesy and downbeat. Clean, blues-infused guitar dominates: cutting through freely without a grounding accompaniment. Die-hard Cave fans will notice this is a re-recording of The Birthday Party's thrashing, noisy original.

'Rye Whiskey' (Trad. Arr. Cave, Harvey) (3:27)
A cover of the traditional folk song, characterised by lilting acoustic guitar and wailing harmonica.

'Running Scared' (Roy Orbison, Joe Melson) (2:06)
This Roy Orbison cover was left off *Kicking Against the Pricks* but was the B-side of 'The Singer'. Like the original, Cave's version is incredibly militaristic, retaining a formal, staccato rhythm throughout, and reaching a sort of climax.

'Black Betty' (Lead Belly) (2:32)
This Lead Belly cover – the other B-side of 'The Singer' – is interesting in that it's mainly just Cave howling *a cappella*. As the song progresses, it becomes more percussive and demented.

'Scum' (Cave, Harvey) (2:53)
This is the infamous song written as a response to the media, whom Cave resented at the time, but it was written particularly with journalist Mat Snow in mind. Having felt betrayed by Snow's review of *The Firstborn Is Dead* and having lived with the man for a while, Cave wrote and released this track on a flexi-disc to be sold at concerts. If anyone doubted this was about Snow, the lines 'black snow' and 'dead snow' negate such thoughts, and there are plenty of other lines that communicate Cave's disapproval of the media.

'The Girl At The Bottom Of My Glass' (4:48)
The B-side of 'Deanna' from the *Tender Prey* sessions, this track follows a 12-bar blues structure, driven by frantic acoustic guitar and the Bad Seeds' slimy wails on the word 'yeah'. Those drunken howls become all the more slimy in the context of the track's parallel to the narrator's wife with his whiskey glass: the source of all his problems, I presume.

'The Train Song' (3:26)
This is a rather sombre lament following the surprise departure of a girl: 'Tell me how long the train's been gone/And was she there?'. A sweet-sounding acoustic guitar drives this, while a beautiful string section adds a romantic colour to this B-side of 'The Ship Song' from *The Good Son*.

'Cocks 'N' Asses' (5:43) (Cave, Victor Van Vugt)
I can see why this B-side of 'The Weeping Song' was left off *The Good Son*, as it definitely would not have fit on there as well as the previous track might've. Weirdly, it's very 1980s in a conventional sense, and is propelled by a drum machine, synths, sinister low-register piano and strange rooster noises. It's an

instrumental, though Cave can be heard mumbling and grumbling. It's a very odd track.

'Blue Bird' (2:46)
The gentle B-side of 'Straight To You'/'Jack The Ripper' from the *Henry's Dream* sessions, this is absent of the trash-can acoustic guitar that characterises the rest of the album. Instead, this murder ballad shines the spotlight on the whiny Hammond organ, and sounds like it could be a *Murder Ballads* B-side, as it is suggested that the narrator kills the blue bird he seems to admire: 'I sent a warning/A warning of disaster', 'I sent that blue bird/Floating down the water'.

'Helpless' (Neil Young) (3:51)
This is from a Neil Young tribute album called *The Bridge* and was also the other B-side of 'The Weeping Song'. Cave's version is languid, and sounds almost hymnal due to the warm church-like organ overtones.

'God's Hotel' (3:07)
This was performed live in a radio session for Santa Monica radio station KCPR, and was released on a compilation of tracks from different artists around the time of *Henry's Dream*. It's a standard 12-bar blues, characterised by playful piano and aggressive slide guitar.

'(I'll Love You) Till The End Of The World' (3:58)
This beautiful love ballad – the B-side of 'Loverman' from the *Let Love In* sessions – sees Cave narrating each verse before falling into a romantic chorus seeped in melodic piano and sweeping strings. In each verse, he concocts a scene of chaos and disrepair in the Longwood hotel, as the narrator escapes an explosion that occurs while he drives away from the event and prays to his lover, who he looks forward to meeting in her 'dress of blue'. Or maybe he didn't escape, and is actually driving towards his lover in Heaven.

'Cassiel's Song' (3:35)
This song was for the film *Faraway, So Close* – Wim Wenders' sequel to *Wings of Desire* – and was also the other B-side of 'Do You Love Me?'. It's incredibly uplifting and reassuring, dominated by piano and soaring strings.

'Tower Of Song' (Leonard Cohen) (5:39)
This is from a 1991 Leonard Cohen tribute album called *I'm Your Fan*. This version first appears rather rollicking and energetic, before it suddenly dies down as Cave practically starts reading Cohen's words like a book. The track is wildly unpredictable, continuing to shift from one groove to the next in an instant.

'What Can I Give You?' (3:40)

Another *Henry's Dream* B-side, the sound here is unconventional in the context of *Henry's* overall brashness. It begins with delicate Rhodes, sweet acoustic guitar and reassuring piano, before a steady drum groove grounds the lyric of adoration: 'Galaxies collide/They shower down around you'. It's got the classic Cave love-ballad sound, although in my opinion the lyrics are a little uninspired.

'What A Wonderful World' (George David Weiss, George Douglas) (3:04)

First performed by Louis Armstrong, this lilting cover is a duet with Cave's friend Shane MacGowan of The Pogues. It has the cheesiness you'd expect from a 1960s pop ballad, complete with strings and oboe. This was released as a single in 1992.

'Rainy Night In Soho' (Shane MacGowan) (3:58)

This MacGowan cover is similarly lilting and oboe-infused. It was included on the 'What A Wonderful World' single.

'Lucy' (Version #2) (2:23)

Originally a track on *The Good Son*, this version is almost identical to the original, except that MacGowan sings the lead vocal. This was also included on the 'What A Wonderful World' single.

'Jack The Ripper' (Acoustic version) (4:45)

Originally a track from *Henry's Dream* released as the B-side of the limited edition 7" of 'Straight to You'/'Jack the Ripper'.

'Sail Away' (4:13)

A rather straightforward lilting love ballad, complete with warbling Hammond organ, gentle vibes and a walking piano line. With optimistic lines like 'Sail away, sail away/To a place where all your troubles can't follow', this *Let Love In* track used as the B-side of 'Do You Love Me?' will have you feeling positive and rejuvenated.

'There's No Night Out In The Jail' (John Harold Ashe) (3:43)

This was recorded in 1993 for a compilation album of Australian country-music covers but was unreleased till now. This cover is perfect for a drunken tavern sing-along.

'That's What Jazz Is To Me' (5:05) (Cave, Harvey, Savage, Wydler)

This is the closest you'll come to hearing the Bad Seeds improvising jazz, and you can certainly tell that nothing had been structured or planned. It's incredibly chaotic, as there's no real sense of tonality in parts, though at other times, a walking bass line allows for some stability. Instruments carelessly dip in and out, contributing to a pot of disorder, while Cave quietly rambles, 'Blind fish being used as musical scales' and 'White blossom falling from the cherry trees' on this amusing *Let Love In* track used as the B-side of 'Red Right Hand'.

'The Willow Garden' (Trad. Arr. Cave, Ellis) (3:59)

Like a few of the tracks on *Murder Ballads*, horrifying murders are framed by a rather languid and serene accompaniment, which somehow makes the crime appear even more chilling. It sounds like a nursery rhyme, with Ellis' playful violin line taking centre stage in the instrumental sections between each verse: in which Conway Savage (not Cave) details Rose Connelly's unhinged murder. In this traditional murder ballad, the narrator poisons and stabs Connelly, throwing her into the river, before he's sent to the gallows for his crime. This is the only Bad Seeds track to feature a lead vocalist other than Cave and was the B-side of 'Where The Wild Roses Grow'.

'The Ballad Of Robert Moore and Betty Coltrane' (3:35)

I will never understand why this wasn't included on *Murder Ballads*. The story is silly but amusing, as three men – including Henry Moore – figure out they've been tricked by Betty Coltrane, who hides under the table of the bar where they confront each other. They all claim to be married to Betty, and Robert Moore shoots the two other men in response before confessing his love to Betty, who he knows is under the table. She then shoots him and robs the three corpses of their money: a tale of love gone wrong. The accompaniment is fast and lively, almost sounding like a sea shanty, once everything has been layered in.

The baritone saxophone really makes the track for me. This was also a B-side of 'Where The Wild Roses Grow'.

'King Kong Kitchee Kitchee Ki-Mi-O' (Trad. Arr. Cave) (3:10)

Another silly B-side from *Murder Ballads*, though this time I'm glad it didn't make the cut and was relegated to the B-side of 'Henry Lee'. It's basically a standard 12-bar blues and a rewriting of a traditional folk ballad in which Mr Frog kills all of Miss Mouse's suitors and marries her. The ridiculous title is repeated like some sort of mantra throughout.

'Knoxville Girl' (Trad. Arr. Cave, Johnston) (3:36)

Another deranged murder takes place here involving a river, and is again framed by a happy accompaniment akin to a nursery rhyme. With just a country acoustic guitar, Cave details the narrator's murder of a Knoxville girl who he beats to a pulp and throws in the river before returning home all bloodied and eventually finding himself in a 'dirty old jail'. This was also a B-side of 'Henry Lee'.

'Where The Wild Roses Grow' (3:47)

This isn't too different to the original, but the main difference is we hear Blixa Bargeld's guide vocal that Kylie Minogue sang for the original.

'O'Malley's Bar Pt. 1' (5:16), 'O'Malley's Bar Pt. 2' (6:38), 'O'Malley's Bar Pt. 3' (4:57)

This was performed for Mark Radcliffe's Radio 1 session but had to be recorded in three parts due to its unconventional length; each part ending with Cave saying, 'Oh my god, he just shot him in the motherfucking head' through a megaphone. He describes this as 'a nutty version of an already nutty song'.

'Time Jesum Transeuntum Et Non Riverentum' (Cave, Ellis, Turner, White) (6:22)

This features Cave and members of The Dirty Three – Ellis' other band that he formed before joining the Bad Seeds. It's a beautiful string-driven piece, included on the 1996 album *Songs in the Key of X: Music from and Inspired by The X-Files* as a hidden track that required listeners to rewind ten minutes before the beginning of the opening track.

'O'Malley's Bar Reprise' (1:03)

Just in case you weren't satisfied with the previous 15 minutes of the Mark Radcliffe version!

'Red Right Hand' (*Scream 3* version) (Cave, Harvey, Wydler) (6:01)

This was augmented for the movie *Scream 3*, and is enhanced with a full orchestra, adding an extra layer of tension and drama.

'Little Empty Boat' (Cave, Bargeld, Casey, Harvey) (4:26)

Harvey believes this should've been used to close *The Boatman's Call* instead of 'Green Eyes'. I disagree, but I can understand how it could work as a closing track. For a record seeped in heartbreak, this track was – according to Cave – unsuitable due to it being too 'comic'. Perhaps the image of the little empty boat that 'don't row, row, row', and the broken oar symbolising a lack of faith or the stagnation of heartbreak, reminded him of the nursery rhyme. It's a little more upbeat than most of the tracks on *The Boatman's Call*: characterised by piano stabs, sprinkles of percussion, and a running bass line. This was a B-side of 'Into My Arms'.

'Right Now, I'm A-Roaming' (Cave, Casey, Harvey, Savage, Wydler) (4:21)

I'd say this is a lot more comic than the previous *The Boatman's Call* B-side. Behind a very simple major chord progression, Cave lists all the rejuvenating, healing things he will do when he arrives home, such as 'clean up my house', 'kick them drugs' and 'see my little boy'. But each verse ends with 'But right now, I am a-roaming' – reminding us that he's yet to do these things, and may never whilst in this state of restlessness. This was also a B-side of 'Into My Arms'.

'Come Into My Sleep' (3:47)
This is a brilliant track used as the B-side of '(Are You) The One That I've Been Waiting For?'. But I can see why it was left off *The Boatman's Call*, as it just doesn't fit the melancholy, down-tempo mood of that album. This is the opposite of both those things – an up-tempo, joyful track in which the narrator yearns for a lost lover to return to him in his sleep. Harvey's skilful vibraphone playing is superb.

'Black Hair' (Band version) (4:13)
Another B-side of '(Are You) The One That I've Been Waiting For?'. The accordion from the original is removed, replaced with the full band here, driven by a steady rhythm section, piano and Hammond organ.

'Babe, I Got You Bad' (3:51)
A very odd B-side, also from the '(Are You) The One That I've Been Waiting For?' single. It sounds nothing like the tracks that made the cut. It's happy, energetic and charged throughout, while the lyrics are rather straightforward and don't need much explanation other than they're full of desire and longing, as the song title suggests.

'Sheep May Safely Graze' (4:14)
Cave wrote this piano-driven song for his son Luke: a sentimental reassurance that everything would be alright. But as a consequence of Bargeld's brutal honesty, it ended up as an outtake: 'Why don't you spare the world this particular masterpiece, and give it to Luke as a gift when he's a little bit older?'. I don't think it's all that bad!

'Opium Tea' (Cave, Savage) (3:48)
Another energetic outtake that thankfully didn't get promoted to anything else. It's not a bad song *per se*, and I find the subject matter relating to the entrapment of drug use interesting. But it just wouldn't fit on *The Boatman's Call* whatsoever.

'Grief Came Riding' (5:05)
This is a typical *No More Shall We Part*-style track in its slow, gentle melancholy dominated by piano and clean, jittering guitar. It was an extra track on that album's limited edition. The lyrics are incredibly depressing, conveying nothing more than hopelessness and despair: 'And if the Thames wasn't so filthy/I'd jump in the river and drown'.

'Bless His Ever Loving Heart' (4:02)
Similar in arrangement, this was also an extra track on the *No More Shall We Part* limited edition. Undoubtedly more uplifting than the previous track, Cave

takes comfort from 'the ever-loving hand' of God in the times 'When it's all come down so hard/And beauty lies exhausted in the street'.

'Good Good Day' (4:04)

Another optimistic track from the *No More Shall We Part* sessions. It's a little more up-tempo. Being next to Mary – who skips and laughs in her dress – seems to be the root of the narrator's happiness, as he repeatedly asserts, 'It's a good, good day today'. This was a B-side of 'As I Sat Sadly By Her Side'.

'Little Janey's Gone' (2:59)

In this final *No More Shall We Part* B-side, we move back to piano-driven melancholy as Cave laments the loss of Little Janey: 'The only one that we could all depend on'. I suppose Little Jancy could be a symbol of anything: a bar; drugs; who knows? This was also a B-side of 'As I Sat Sadly By Her Side'.

'I Feel So Good' (J. B. Lenoir) (1:44)

A 12-bar blues performed for Wim Wenders' 2003 documentary *The Soul of a Man*.

'Shoot Me Down' (3:32)

The B-side of 'Bring It On' from *Nocturama* continues the muted, sombre mood and arrangements of the previous two albums. Though the romantic lyrics are rather uninspired, I prefer this to some of the tracks that made it onto the album.

'Swing Low' (5:40)

I can't understand how *this* didn't make the cut, but somehow 'Bring It On' – the single it's the B-side of – found its way onto *Nocturama*. Characterised by guitar volume swells, Hammond organ flutters and splutters, and jangling guitar, it's an exercise in tension and dynamics.

'Little Ghost Song' (3:44)

This B-side of 'He Wants You'/'Babe, I'm On Fire' is a remixed version of 'Right Out Of My Hand' from *Nocturama*.

'Everything Must Converge' (3:17)

There's nothing special at all about this B-side of 'He Wants You'/'Babe, I'm On Fire'. It's rather dull, and the title is the only message.

'Nocturama' (4:01)

The proposed title track of *Nocturama* was relegated to the B-side of a limited edition 7" of 'Rock Of Gibraltar', and for good reason. Again, there's nothing worthy of explanation. It's an average down-tempo love song.

'She's Leaving You' (Cave, Ellis, Casey, Sclavunos) (4:01)

You can really hear the difference going from the tired *Nocturama* B-sides to the immeasurable potency of the *Abattoir/Lyre* B-sides: this one being the B-side of 'Nature Boy'. This is a raucous call for some sort of relief as the narrator battles his insecurity and struggles to trust his lover, who he believes will leave him. Though it is incredibly frantic and captivating, it's not as unique as its superiors.

'Under This Moon' (4:01)

This grandiose collection closes with a second *Abattoir/Lyre* B-side from the 'Breathless'/'There She Goes, My Beautiful World' single. It's upbeat and cheery despite the subject matter, which I cannot fathom. We are presented with a couple that at times could be happy, but at others, something seems off: 'Your lover just called/He's on the phone/I'm telling him kindly that you're not alone'. Whatever is or isn't wrong, being under the moon with his lover provides comfort.

Lovely Creatures: The Best of Nick Cave & The Bad Seeds (2017)

A second compilation of some of the band's greatest hits, curated by Cave and Harvey. It covers a whopping 30-year career, moving from *From Her to Eternity* right through to *Push the Sky Away*. Cave says this about it on his website:

> There are some people out there who just don't know where to start with The Bad Seeds. Others know the catalogue better than I do! This release is designed to be a way into three decades of music-making. That's a lot of songs. The songs we have chosen are the ones that have stuck around, for whatever reason. Some songs are those that demand to be played live. Others are lesser songs that are personal favourites of ours. Others are just too big and have too much history to leave out. And there are those that didn't make it, poor things. They are the ones you must discover by yourselves.

For a beginner, this is the perfect entry point into Cave's rather daunting back catalogue, and this time, the tracks are in chronological order (except for the vinyl version, which also has a reduced tracklist).

B-sides & Rarities Part II (2021)

This is the second part of the infamous 2005 box set, and was released in 2021 along with a reissue of part one. These 27 tracks complete the band's current tenure of albums from *Dig, Lazarus, Dig!!!* onwards, and it was curated by Cave and second-in-command Warren Ellis. The bulk of the tracks are B-sides, but there are some reinterpretations of older tracks, a couple of covers, and even a few working versions. This ultimately closes a chapter on a period of the Bad Seeds in which Ellis has dominated most. Whatever happens next, Ellis will probably still be a dominant figure in the band, and hopefully, at some point, there will be a part three to the *B-sides & Rarities* album!

'Hey Little Firing Squad' (4:00)
This is a straightforward and melodic *Dig, Lazarus, Dig!!!* B-side from the single 'Midnight Man'. It seems to portray a couple in the throes of an idyllic relationship: 'I woke up early this morning/I was covered in sleeping kids/ And then I reached out for my woman/All twisted in the sheets'. The drunk-sounding chorus perhaps represents the relationship's permanent cheer.

'Fleeting Love' (4:18)
This piano and guitar-driven love ballad from the *Dig, Lazarus, Dig!!!* sessions was the B-side of 'More News From Nowhere', and details exactly what the title suggests. I believe the narrator is cheating on his lover, who he once confessed his 'undying love' for in 'the Stone age'. But this was just a phase, as he finds new life in meeting new lovers: 'Darling, don't you sigh/'Cause everybody needs some fleeting love'.

'Accidents Will Happen' (4:19)
The lighthearted, comic B-side of the 'Dig, Lazarus, Dig!!!' single is driven by clean, jangling guitar. The song is rather petty, as the narrator wishes for an 'accident' to happen to his ex-lover's new husband whilst also falling into the lustful trap of having repeated dalliances with his ex-lover, which he terms as 'accidents'. It's not the best song in the world, and I'm glad it didn't make the cut, though, in an unconventional twist, Cave plays an actual guitar solo, which can certainly be called interesting.

'Free To Walk' (featuring Debbie Harry) (3:08)
This acoustic bluegrass duet between Cave and Debbie Harry was for *We Are Only Riders: The Jeffrey Lee Pierce Sessions Project* – a compilation album of lost songs by founding member of The Gun Club Jeffrey Lee Pierce, brought to life by a cast of musicians.

'Avalanche' (Cohen) (4:34)
Cave opened the Bad Seeds' career with a more-demented version of this Leonard Cohen song, on *From Her to Eternity*. This version recorded in 2015 for the second season of the television series *Black Sails*, is even more fragile than Cohen's original. Accompanied by piano and a mournful violin, Cave delivers the lyrics with a tenderness absent from his initial cover.

'Vortex' (4:38)
This up-tempo track recorded in 2006 by Cave, Ellis, Sclavunos and Casey remained unreleased because 'The band were never able to define the song as either Grinderman or Bad Seeds'. For me, it lacks the punch of both bands,

and it was probably wise it found a home here. It's an average rock song, though there are some lovely pizzicato strings in the background.

'Needle Boy' (3:54)

Powered by an isolated robotic drone that often sounds clanky, this *Push the Sky Away* outtake released as a single in 2013, details Cave's recovery from heroin addiction 'at the turn of the century'. In order to protect himself from this evil addiction, he takes superstitious precautions and hides a plethora of voodoo dolls that each symbolise some sort of evil. In the song's second half, these figurines take on a life of their own, as they do what they were intended to do – protect Cave from the evil that arrives in his room – by the end, he's dancing on the rooftops in celebration.

'Lightning Bolts' (3:49)

This is a very unsettling piece of music, which relies on Ellis' interleaved, jittering loops. In fact, it's like being stuck in a tornado of static, which probably reflects the tumultuous state of Greece at the time. Cave once again turns to mythology as a way of communicating the destruction in Greece:

> My lightning bolts are jolts of joy
> They are joy boys from Zeus
> I feed them porridge in their booster seats of knowledge
> And in the cradle of democracy
> The pigeons are wearing gas masks

Zeus and his lightning bolts represent the destruction imposed by austerity in Athens – a city once known as 'the cradle of democracy', clouded in a haze of gas that's so choking, even 'the pigeons are wearing gas masks'. It's discomforting yet arousing in its message. This was included on the 'Needle Boy' single.

'Animal X' (3:51)

This was a single for Record Store Day 2013 and is similarly unsettled by Ellis' interleaving violin loops. A steady drum rhythm at least allows for some stability as Cave narrates a rambling story about the meeting of animal x with animal y. These individuals represent all of humanity, who are described in terms of primal instinct rather than individual personality – made for each other in the sense that they both possess the body of a human: 'Bit by bit, and piece by piece/They were built for each other, by some cosmic hand'. But these individuals are stripped of emotion, and are missing the vital parts that allow us to perform daily activities; Cave renders humanity as meaningless and aimless.

'Give Us A Kiss' (3:34)

Another *Push the Sky Away* B-side, which was first revealed in the 2014 documentary *20,000 Days on Earth*: directed by Jane Pollard and Ian Forsyth.

The film version is just Cave and piano: a beautiful rendition that I prefer to this one. That's not to say that this more floaty cinematic version led by the gentle throbbing of strings is any less worthy; on the contrary – I think it should've made it onto the album. The high-pitched quivering of Ellis' violin mirrors the screaming lustful desires of Cave's youth: 'And you're still hanging out in my dreams/In your sister's shoes and your blue jeans/Give us a kiss'.

'Push The Sky Away' (Live with the Melbourne Symphony Orchestra) (5:20)
It's a popular thing for an artist to reimagine their songs with an orchestra, as there's nothing quite like the rich decadence of such a sound. This version is no exception – recorded while Cave and Ellis were touring music from their film soundtracks.

'First Skeleton Tree' (3:05)
This initial version of 'Skeleton Tree' feels a lot less hopeful about the future compared to the original, which is at least given warmth through the synths and a stable, steady drum rhythm. This version floats in a state of misery, as a mournful piano replaces those warm synths, and there is *no* stability; everything feels more empty here.

'King Sized Nick Cave Blues' (3:53)
This piano-led product of the *Skeleton Tree* sessions is not as grief-centred, or at least not in the same way, as here Cave laments the younger, less-famous version of himself:

> These king-sized tears do not come free but beyond me
> Drowning my eyes with floods of unexpected memories
> Of a time of wanting, wanting it all, wanting everything

There is a dichotomy between the real Nick Cave, who wants the 'everything that eventually kills', and the 'king-sized shadow' he's attached to, saying 'hello' to one and 'goodbye' to another. The lyrics first appeared in *The Sick Bag Song*: a 2015 Cave book that revealed his inner thoughts written down on sick bags whilst journeying around North America on the 2014 Bad Seeds tour.

'Opium Eyes' (2:27)
The low, menacing rumble of this pulsing *Skeleton Tree* outtake reminds me of songs like 'Jesus Alone' and 'Anthrocene', which did make the cut. Like a few of the *Skeleton Tree* songs, it communicates violent desires: 'He started killing men and he ain't well/Scattered their bones across the sky': a morbid way of saying he sent them to their maker. Cave parallels himself with this murderer ('He kept moving and so did I/And flew clear and so did I'), or maybe they are the same person. Or maybe the song title refers to

the opposite of rose-tinted glasses, and through the eyes of trauma, Cave becomes an individual with murderous desires.

'Big Dream (With Sky)' (3:27)

This *Ghosteen* outtake begins with the horrifying image of a giant with a 'Green triangulated head and bulging eyes', and then transitions into something rather euphoric as Cave and a chorus of Ellis' backing vocals repeat a sort of onomatopoeic figure which arrives on each repetition like waves of an ocean. Trying to glean some meaning from this is tricky, but it is beautiful nonetheless.

'Instrumental #33' (2:26)

An instrumental recorded during the *Skeleton Tree* period. A synthesizer bell sound drives the track, playing in constant triplets while a weaker synth accompanies.

'Hell Villanelle' (3:49)

Another *Skeleton Tree* outtake, with an eerie pulsating rumble. There isn't much hope in a line like 'There's more paradise in hell than we've been told'. Perhaps it refers to a longing to commit aggressive, violent acts in the face of trauma; a desire to be hellish in a world that appears hellish in the throes of immediate trauma. But Cave's ambiguous lyrics are subject to interpretation.

'Euthanasia' (2:47)

A solemn *Skeleton Tree* outtake that showcases the sole power of Cave and a piano. He first performed this on the live-streamed concert film *Idiot Prayer: Nick Cave Alone at Alexandra Palace,* and I remember being captivated by the lyrics, which communicate a deep alienation from the world in the face of trauma ('And in looking for you/I lost myself in time'), which is eventually resolved by the smiling person he finds sitting at the kitchen table, who I believe to be Susie. Perhaps such resolution wasn't appropriate for an album as devastating as *Skeleton Tree.*

'Life Per Se' (2:59)

This *Skeleton Tree* outtake is beautiful, driven by piano and Ellis' wearied, screeching backing vocals. Ultimately it was deemed too sad for the album. Cave asserts he has nothing against life *per se,* but morbidly, 'There is always the little stuff to stop the big stuff/Making you wanna shoot yourself in the head'. For Cave, Susie represents the 'little stuff', providing respite from the 'big stuff': a reference to all of the world's injustice and suffering. The line 'I slide my little songs out from under you' appears in the *Ghosteen* song 'Night Raid', but was in this B-side first to communicate the small respite Cave receives from having Susie as a creative inspiration.

'Steve McQueen' (3:49)

This spoken-word outtake from the *Skeleton Tree* sessions was first heard in Andrew Dominik's accompanying documentary film *One More Time with Feeling*. Cave's ramblings are accompanied by a lone synth which plays the piano melody from 'Girl in Amber'. Like many of the *Skeleton Tree* lyrics, this is in a stream-of-consciousness style, contrasting images of despair ('But mostly I curl up inside my typewriter with my housefly and cry/I tell my housefly not to cry/My housefly tells me not to die') with images of anger and violence ('Sometimes I get the elevator to the top of the Burj Al Arab/And shoot my guns across Dubai/Bang, bang, bang, I'm that kinda guy'), which succeed in communicating grief in its immediacy.

'First Bright Horses' (2:35)

This is very different to how it eventually sounded. It's stripped of piano, slower, dreamier and almost completely synth-driven. The lyrics – in their incomplete state – reflect this happier sound, as the wonder of the imagination is not undermined like on the original. Instead, 'the wide windows of wonder are jammed' and can't be closed.

'First Girl in Amber' (2:59)

The first small idea for this song is also more dreamy than the original, existing in a sort of limbo. There is less purpose here, everything floats a little more, and it doesn't sound as broken as the original. I really admire the majestic middle section; such a shame this musical idea never made it onto a different A-side track.

'Glacier' (2:39)

This reflective instrumental from the *Push the Sky Away* sessions somehow feels quite nostalgic to me – I'm not sure why. The serene atmosphere that Ellis can create with a loop, which elegantly dances around Cave's gentle piano tinkles, takes me back to a happy time of childhood wonder and fascination. A beautiful little track.

'Heart That Kills You' (3:05)

Here is a strange retelling of the fall of Adam and Eve, in which, 'like a little apple', they drop from paradise into L.A., dropping from the sky down towards the mortal world. Cave warns of the perils of loving something and the repercussions of loving something that you lose. Like Adam and Eve, Cave and Susie had to move from Brighton – the place of their son's death – to L.A, to escape from their grief. But with grief still biting into them like serpents, they moved back to Brighton, because, 'In the end, it is your heart that kills you' – the home of love where grief is most felt, and therefore, trying to escape from grief is futile. Cave wrote this during the *Ghosteen* sessions, not long after his son's death.

'First Waiting for You' (1:41)

This fragment isn't too different from the original; the main difference being the relentless repetition of the percussive industrial pulse: which fades out as the piano comes in on the original, but perseveres here.

'Sudden Song' (1:41)

This brief but uplifting outtake from the *Skeleton Tree* sessions feels quite heavenly. The lyrics are tricky to grasp, being in a stream-of-consciousness. But I think the narrator is departing from his lover on 'a jet plane', leaving the bridge between them 'burned down' due to their separation.

'Earthlings' (3:00)

This final B-side is one taken from *Ghosteen*, and the lyrics are very similar to 'Ghosteen Speaks':

> I thought these ghosts were there to set me free
> I thought these songs had travelled here for me
> I think they're singing to be free

Perhaps this was written before 'Ghosteen' was a part of the album, and it's interesting to see how these lyrics began. Framing it is the sparse backdrop of a lone synth, bass and gentle celeste twinkles. Later on, the ghosts Cave outlines become a chorus of voices repeating 'Oombaya, oh Lord': a breathtaking end to a wonderful album of lost songs.

Bibliography

Essential Reading
Cave, N., *The Complete Lyrics 1978-2013* (Penguin Books, 2013)
Cave, N., *And the Ass Saw the Angel* (Black Spring Press, 1989)
Cave, N., *The Death of Bunny Munro* (Canongate Books, 2009)
Johnston, I., *Bad Seed: The Biography of Nick Cave* (Little, Brown & Company, 1995)
Mordue, M., *Boy on Fire: The Young Nick Cave* (Allen & Unwin, 2021)
Snow, M. (ed.), *Nick Cave – Sinner Saint: The True Confessions* (Plexus Publishing, 2011)

Online Resources
ianandjane.com – website containing 14 short films titled 'Do You Love Me Like I Love You?'; directed by Ian Forsyth and Jane Pollard.
nickcave.com – official Nick Cave Website.
rocksbackpages.com – website containing countless Bad Seeds album and live reviews and interviews.
theredhandfiles.com – Cave's Q&A 2ebsite

Visual and Audio Resources
20,000 Days on Earth, directed by Ian Forsyth and Jane Pollard (Picturehouse Entertainment, 2014).
Cave, N., *The Secret Life Of The Love Song & The Flesh Made Word: Two Lectures By Nick Cave* (Mute Records, 2000). Initially written for BBC Radio 3 religious services, 1996.
One More Time with Feeling, directed by Andrew Dominik (Trafalgar Releases, 2016)

Roy Harper - *on track*
every album, every song

Opher Goodwin
Paperback
160 pages
50 colour photographs
978-1-78951-130-6
£14.99
$21.95

**Every album and
every song by
this legendary
troubadour.**

Roy Harper must be one of Britain's most undervalued rock musicians and songwriters. For over fifty years, he has produced a series of innovative albums of consistently outstanding quality, putting poetry and social commentary to music in a way that extends the boundaries of rock music. His 22 studio albums and 16 live albums, made up of 250 songs, have created a unique body of work.

Roy is a musician's musician. He is lauded by the likes of Dave Gilmour, Ian Anderson, Jimmy Page, Pete Townsend, Joanna Newsom, Fleet Foxes and Kate Bush. Who else could boast that he has had Keith Moon, Jimmy Page, Dave Gilmour, John Paul Jones, Ronnie Lane, Chris Spedding, Bill Bruford and Steve Broughton in his backing band? Notable albums include *Stormcock*, *HQ* and *Bullinamingvase*.

Opher Goodwin, Roy's friend and a fan, guides the reader through every album and song, providing insight into the recording of the songs as well the times in which they were recorded. As his loyal and often fanatical fans will attest, Roy has produced a series of epic songs and he remains a raging, uncompromising individual.

Laura Nyro - *on track*
every album, every song

Philip Ward
Paperback
160 pages
42 colour photographs
978-1-78951-182-5
£15.99
$22.95

**Every album and
every song by this
legendary American
singer-songwriter.**

Laura Nyro (1947-1997) was one of the most significant figures to emerge from the singer-songwriter boom of the 1960s. She first came to attention when her songs were hits for Barbra Streisand, The Fifth Dimension, Peter, Paul and Mary, and others. But it was on her own recordings that she imprinted her vibrant personality. With albums like Eli and the Thirteenth Confession and New York Tendaberry she mixed the sounds of soul, pop, jazz and Broadway to fashion autobiographical songs that earned her a fanatical following and influenced a generation of music-makers. In later life her preoccupations shifted from the self to embrace public causes such as feminism, animal rights and ecology – the music grew mellower, but her genius was undimmed.

This book examines her entire studio career from 1967's More than a New Discovery to the posthumous Angel in the Dark release of 2001. Also surveyed are the many live albums that preserve her charismatic stage presence. With analysis of her teasing, poetic lyrics and unique vocal and harmonic style, this is the first-ever study to concentrate on Laura Nyro's music and how she created it. Elton John idolised her; Joni Mitchell declared her 'a complete original'. Here's why.

Warren Zevon - *on track*
every album, every song

Peter Gallagher
Paperback
128 pages
40 colour photographs
978-1-78951-170-2
£15.99
$22.95

Every album and every song by this underappreciated American songwriter.

Bruce Springsteen called him 'one of the great, great American songwriters', Jackson Browne hailed him as 'the first and foremost proponent of song noir' and Stephen King once said that if he could write like Zevon, he 'would be a happy guy'. The list of artists that lined up to appear on his records include Springsteen, Neil Young, Bob Dylan, Dave Gilmour and Emmylou Harris. So how is it that most people, if they have heard of Warren Zevon at all, know him only as 'that werewolves guy'?

This book goes beyond that solitary hit single to examine all aspects of Zevon's multifaceted, five-decade career, from his beginnings in the slightly psychedelic folk duo Lyme and Cybelle, through to his commercial breakthrough in the late Seventies with *Excitable Boy*, his critically acclaimed late Eighties comeback *Sentimental Hygiene*, his decline into cult obscurity, and his triumphant if heart-breaking final testament *The Wind* released just prior to his death in 2003.

Along the way, the reader will discover one of rock's consummate balladeers, as well as his cast of characters, which include doomed drug dealers, psychopathic adolescents, outlaws of the Old West, BDSM fetishists, ghostly gunslingers and, yes, lycanthropes unleashed on the streets of London.

On Track series

Alan Parsons Project – Steve Swift 978-1-78952-154-2
Tori Amos – Lisa Torem 978-1-78952-142-9
Asia – Peter Braidis 978-1-78952-099-6
Badfinger – Robert Day-Webb 978-1-878952-176-4
Barclay James Harvest – Keith and Monica Domone 978-1-78952-067-5
The Beatles – Andrew Wild 978-1-78952-009-5
The Beatles Solo 1969-1980 – Andrew Wild 978-1-78952-030-9
Blue Oyster Cult – Jacob Holm-Lupo 978-1-78952-007-1
Blur – Matt Bishop – 978-178952-164-1
Marc Bolan and T.Rex – Peter Gallagher 978-1-78952-124-5
Kate Bush – Bill Thomas 978-1-78952-097-2
Camel – Hamish Kuzminski 978-1-78952-040-8
Caravan – Andy Boot 978-1-78952-127-6
Cardiacs – Eric Benac 978-1-78952-131-3
Eric Clapton Solo – Andrew Wild 978-1-78952-141-2
The Clash – Nick Assirati 978-1-78952-077-4
Crosby, Stills and Nash – Andrew Wild 978-1-78952-039-2
The Damned – Morgan Brown 978-1-78952-136-8
Deep Purple and Rainbow 1968-79 – Steve Pilkington 978-1-78952-002-6
Dire Straits – Andrew Wild 978-1-78952-044-6
The Doors – Tony Thompson 978-1-78952-137-5
Dream Theater – Jordan Blum 978-1-78952-050-7
Electric Light Orchestra – Barry Delve 978-1-78952-152-8
Elvis Costello and The Attractions – Georg Purvis 978-1-78952-129-0
Emerson Lake and Palmer – Mike Goode 978-1-78952-000-2
Fairport Convention – Kevan Furbank 978-1-78952-051-4
Peter Gabriel – Graeme Scarfe 978-1-78952-138-2
Genesis – Stuart MacFarlane 978-1-78952-005-7
Gentle Giant – Gary Steel 978-1-78952-058-3
Gong – Kevan Furbank 978-1-78952-082-8
Hall and Oates – Ian Abrahams 978-1-78952-167-2
Hawkwind – Duncan Harris 978-1-78952-052-1
Peter Hammill – Richard Rees Jones 978-1-78952-163-4
Roy Harper – Opher Goodwin 978-1-78952-130-6
Jimi Hendrix – Emma Stott 978-1-78952-175-7
The Hollies – Andrew Darlington 978-1-78952-159-7
Iron Maiden – Steve Pilkington 978-1-78952-061-3
Jefferson Airplane – Richard Butterworth 978-1-78952-143-6
Jethro Tull – Jordan Blum 978-1-78952-016-3
Elton John in the 1970s – Peter Kearns 978-1-78952-034-7
The Incredible String Band – Tim Moon 978-1-78952-107-8
Iron Maiden – Steve Pilkington 978-1-78952-061-3
Judas Priest – John Tucker 978-1-78952-018-7

Kansas – Kevin Cummings 978-1-78952-057-6
The Kinks – Martin Hutchinson 978-1-78952-172-6
Korn – Matt Karpe 978-1-78952-153-5
Led Zeppelin – Steve Pilkington 978-1-78952-151-1
Level 42 – Matt Philips 978-1-78952-102-3
Little Feat – 978-1-78952-168-9
Aimee Mann – Jez Rowden 978-1-78952-036-1
Joni Mitchell – Peter Kearns 978-1-78952-081-1
The Moody Blues – Geoffrey Feakes 978-1-78952-042-2
Motorhead – Duncan Harris 978-1-78952-173-3
Mike Oldfield – Ryan Yard 978-1-78952-060-6
Opeth – Jordan Blum 978-1-78-952-166-5
Tom Petty – Richard James 978-1-78952-128-3
Porcupine Tree – Nick Holmes 978-1-78952-144-3
Queen – Andrew Wild 978-1-78952-003-3
Radiohead – William Allen 978-1-78952-149-8
Renaissance – David Detmer 978-1-78952-062-0
The Rolling Stones 1963-80 – Steve Pilkington 978-1-78952-017-0
The Smiths and Morrissey – Tommy Gunnarsson 978-1-78952-140-5
Status Quo the Frantic Four Years – Richard James 978-1-78952-160-3
Steely Dan – Jez Rowden 978-1-78952-043-9
Steve Hackett – Geoffrey Feakes 978-1-78952-098-9
Thin Lizzy – Graeme Stroud 978-1-78952-064-4
Toto – Jacob Holm-Lupo 978-1-78952-019-4
U2 – Eoghan Lyng 978-1-78952-078-1
UFO – Richard James 978-1-78952-073-6
The Who – Geoffrey Feakes 978-1-78952-076-7
Roy Wood and the Move – James R Turner 978-1-78952-008-8
Van Der Graaf Generator – Dan Coffey 978-1-78952-031-6
Yes – Stephen Lambe 978-1-78952-001-9
Frank Zappa 1966 to 1979 – Eric Benac 978-1-78952-033-0
Warren Zevon – Peter Gallagher 978-1-78952-170-2
10CC – Peter Kearns 978-1-78952-054-5

Decades Series

The Bee Gees in the 1960s – Andrew Mon Hughes et al 978-1-78952-148-1
The Bee Gees in the 1970s – Andrew Mon Hughes et al 978-1-78952-179-5
Black Sabbath in the 1970s – Chris Sutton 978-1-78952-171-9
Britpop – Peter Richard Adams and Matt Pooler 978-1-78952-169-6
Alice Cooper in the 1970s – Chris Sutton 978-1-78952-104-7
Curved Air in the 1970s – Laura Shenton 978-1-78952-069-9
Bob Dylan in the 1980s – Don Klees 978-1-78952-157-3
Fleetwood Mac in the 1970s – Andrew Wild 978-1-78952-105-4
Focus in the 1970s – Stephen Lambe 978-1-78952-079-8
Free and Bad Company in the 1970s – John Van der Kiste 978-1-78952-178-8

Genesis in the 1970s – Bill Thomas 978178952-146-7
George Harrison in the 1970s – Eoghan Lyng 978-1-78952-174-0
Marillion in the 1980s – Nathaniel Webb 978-1-78952-065-1
Mott the Hoople and Ian Hunter in the 1970s – John Van der Kiste
978-1-78-952-162-7
Pink Floyd In The 1970s – Georg Purvis 978-1-78952-072-9
Tangerine Dream in the 1970s – Stephen Palmer 978-1-78952-161-0
The Sweet in the 1970s – Darren Johnson 978-1-78952-139-9
Uriah Heep in the 1970s – Steve Pilkington 978-1-78952-103-0
Yes in the 1980s – Stephen Lambe with David Watkinson 978-1-78952-125-2

On Screen series
Carry On... – Stephen Lambe 978-1-78952-004-0
David Cronenberg – Patrick Chapman 978-1-78952-071-2
Doctor Who: The David Tennant Years – Jamie Hailstone 978-1-78952-066-8
James Bond – Andrew Wild – 978-1-78952-010-1
Monty Python – Steve Pilkington 978-1-78952-047-7
Seinfeld Seasons 1 to 5 – Stephen Lambe 978-1-78952-012-5

Other Books
1967: A Year In Psychedelic Rock – Kevan Furbank 978-1-78952-155-9
1970: A Year In Rock – John Van der Kiste 978-1-78952-147-4
1973: The Golden Year of Progressive Rock 978-1-78952-165-8
Babysitting A Band On The Rocks – G.D. Praetorius 978-1-78952-106-1
Eric Clapton Sessions – Andrew Wild 978-1-78952-177-1
Derek Taylor: For Your Radioactive Children – Andrew Darlington
978-1-78952-038-5
The Golden Road: The Recording History of The Grateful Dead – John Kilbride
978-1-78952-156-6
Iggy and The Stooges On Stage 1967-1974 – Per Nilsen 978-1-78952-101-6
Jon Anderson and the Warriors – the road to Yes – David Watkinson
978-1-78952-059-0
Nu Metal: A Definitive Guide – Matt Karpe 978-1-78952-063-7
Tommy Bolin: In and Out of Deep Purple – Laura Shenton 978-1-78952-070-5
Maximum Darkness – Deke Leonard 978-1-78952-048-4
Maybe I Should've Stayed In Bed – Deke Leonard 978-1-78952-053-8
The Twang Dynasty – Deke Leonard 978-1-78952-049-1

and many more to come!

Would you like to write for Sonicbond Publishing?
We are mainly a music publisher, but we also occasionally
publish in other genres including film and television. At Sonicbond
Publishing we are always on the look-out for authors, particularly for
our two main series, On Track and Decades.

Mixing fact with in depth analysis, the On Track series examines
the entire recorded work of a particular musical artist or group. All
genres are considered from easy listening and jazz to 60s soul to 90s
pop, via rock and metal.

The Decades series singles out a particular decade in an artist or
group's history and focuses on that decade in more detail than may
be allowed in the On Track series.

While professional writing experience would, of course, be
an advantage, the most important qualification is to have real
enthusiasm and knowledge of your subject. First-time authors are
welcomed, but the ability to write well in English is essential.

Sonicbond Publishing has distribution throughout Europe and
North America, and all our books are also published in E-book form.
Authors will be paid a royalty based on sales of their book.
Further details about our books are available from
www.sonicbondpublishing.com. To contact us, complete the
contact form there or email info@sonicbondpublishing.co.uk